Traditional Witchcraft and the Pagan Revival

A Magical Anthropology

Traditional Witchcraft and the Pagan Revival

A Magical Anthropology

Mélusine Draco

MOON
BOOKS

Winchester, UK
Washington, USA

First published by Moon Books, 2013
Moon Books is an imprint of John Hunt Publishing Ltd., Laurel House, Station Approach,
Alresford, Hants, SO24 9JH, UK
office1@jhpbooks.net
www.johnhuntpublishing.com
www.moon-books.net

For distributor details and how to order please visit the 'Ordering' section on our website.

Text copyright: Mélusine Draco 2013

ISBN: 978 1 78279 156 0

A CIP catalogue record for this book is available from the British Library.

Design: Stuart Davies

Printed and bound by CPI Group (UK) Ltd, Croydon, CR0 4YY

We operate a distinctive and ethical publishing philosophy in all areas of our business, from our global network of authors to production and worldwide distribution.

CONTENTS

Chapter titles from music by George Henry Crumb, USA

Dedicated to Alan Richardson and Michael Howard who
keep everyone's feet firmly on the ground …

About the Author

Mélusine Draco originally trained in the magical arts of traditional British Old Craft with Bob and Mériém Clay-Egerton. She has been a magical and spiritual instructor for over 20 years with Arcanum and the Temple of Khem, and writer of numerous popular books on magic and witchcraft. Her highly individualistic teaching methods and writing draw on ancient sources, supported by academic texts and current archaeological findings. www.covenofthescales.com.

Her *Traditional Witchcraft* series is published by Moon Books (an imprint of John Hunt Publishing): *Traditional Witchcraft for Urban Living, Traditional Witchcraft for the Seashore, Traditional Witchcraft for Fields and Hedgerows* and *Traditional Witchcraft for Woods and Forests. Traditional Witchcraft and Modern Paganism* is the fifth book in the series. *The Dictionary of Mystery & Magic, By Spellbook & Candle* and *Magic Crystals, Sacred Stones* (Axis Mundi) are also available from John Hunt Publishing imprints.

Introduction

The aim of *Traditional Witchcraft and the Pagan Revival* is to provide a sympathetic approach to the evolution of witchcraft as a historical reality, rather than as mere circumspection – or wishful thinking. By combining scholarly writing and recent archaeological findings with a 'quality of fascination', I hope it will prove to be a delight to read and a source of new insight for those who would follow the traditions of the Old Ways. It shows that witchcraft did (and does) exist, and traces the origins and true nature of the many different contemporary pagan beliefs back to their roots. And, what is equally as important, to understand *when* outside foreign influences were grafted onto indigenous pagan stock.

Generally speaking, today's paganism falls into four different elements, which in turn separate the different approaches and levels of magical practice. A considerable amount of magical writing can be incomprehensible to those who have not been schooled in that particular path or tradition – so we begin at the beginning and work ourselves up through the spheres of **Knowledge, Wisdom** and **Understanding**. And we start by accepting that there *is* a divide between the various approaches to paganism and magical practice. Such as:

- **Animistic:** The belief that everything animate and inanimate has its own life-force, such as that which forms the basis of shamanism and Old Craft;
- **Eclectic:** Selecting or borrowing from a variety of styles, systems, theories, beliefs, etc., as commonly found in modern paganism and Wicca;
- **Syncretic:** The attempt to reconcile different systems of belief; the fusion or blending of religions, as by identification of gods, taking over of observances, or selection of

whatever seems best in each; often producing a seemingly illogical compromise in belief. Found in many aspects of Western Ritual Magic, and the initiatory branches of traditional witchcraft;

- **Synergetic**: Combined or co-ordinated action; increased effect of two elements obtained by using them together. The combining of ancient wisdom with modern magical applications, as in the case of the contemporary approaches of Old Craft, Norse (Heathen) and Druidry.

As I observed in *Coven of the Scales: The Collected Writings of A R Clay-Egerton*, it should be understood that although Bob and Mériém Clay-Egerton firmly held the philosophy and opinion that all faiths were one, and that all paths led to the same goal, they did *not* advocate what is now referred to as 'eclectic' paganism. What they *did* teach was the desire for knowledge and experience, regardless of source. **Each new experience was studied within the confines of that particular religion, path or tradition. Each discipline was kept completely separate from another.** Only when a student had a *thorough* understanding of the tenets of each discipline were they encouraged to formulate them into their own individual system.

These sentiments were echoed by Dion Fortune in *The Mystical Qabalah*:

No student will ever make any progress in spiritual development who flits from system to system; first using some New Thought affirmations, then some Yoga breathing-exercises and meditation-postures, and following these by an attempt at the mystical methods of prayer. Each of these systems has its value, but that value can only be realised if the system is carried out in its entirety ... the student who sets out to be an eclectic before he has made himself an expert will never be anything more than a dabbler.

This book invites the reader to take the opportunity to step back in time and discover – through the gateways of intuition and instinct – where their own individual roots can be found.

Mélusine Draco – Winter Solstice 2012

Chapter One

Echoes of Time and the River (Prologue)

One of the most striking features of the history of all religion is the way in which people have clung to the holy places of their far-off ancestors. It appears that once a site was sanctified through worship, an incoming people whether aggressive invaders, or the peaceful missionaries, gained prestige by occupying the site. When this was done, the old religion could be overthrown and the area purified with new ritual and religious observance.
Readers Digest, *Folklore, Myths and Legends of Britain*

When we read about ancestral British paganism today, more often than not, it is tinged with the rosy hue of the noble savage and wishful thinking, rather than based on progressive archaeological or anthropological discovery. For the first half-million years after our pre-human ancestors slowly morphed into a recognisable form, they were still primitives who left relatively little evidence of their existence except for a few bones and Palaeolithic tools. The emergence from the hunter-gatherer era to the development of agriculture, the domestication of animals, pottery and weaving, is a mere 10,000 years ago; while 'civilisation' as we understand it, only dates back some 5,000 years.

Unfortunately, in the rush to establish the many different forms of 20th century revivalist paganism, the element of curiosity has often been suppressed in favour of historical ignorance. Anything that is non-Christian in origin is immediately embraced as 'pagan', despite the fact that much of it had little to do with the indigenous people of the British Isles. It also leads to the acceptance of 'fakelore and fantasy' as the basis for a considerable amount of contemporary thinking. Reviewing one of these pseudo-history books in *White Dragon* magazine some years ago, the editor wrote: 'Books like this pose more of a danger to paganism than the Christian Right will ever do, because they are the enemy within, subverting the Mysteries and dumbing down for spirituality's equivalent of the day-time television audience.' Ouch!

Never before, however, in the entire history of religion, have ancient beliefs been so popular, or so socially acceptable. For some time now, there have been organisations campaigning for governmental recognition of 'paganism' as a legitimate form of religion or worship, despite the opinions of many of the old brigade, that paganism *per se* is *not* a religion but an umbrella term for a wide variety of loosely linked modern revivalist 'traditions' or 'paths'. In *The New Believers*, a book covering 'sects, cults and alternative religions', David V. Barrett is not wide off the mark in describing the contemporary esoteric pagan scene in the following terms:

Some are a synthesis of Western (Judaeo-Christian) and Eastern (Hindu, Buddhist or Sufi) thought; others could be described as mystical, magical, Judaeo-Christianity. Many believe in Secret Masters who have tremendous powers and who have guarded the true religious teaching ... Some are, in one way or another Gnostic, in that they emphasise secret knowledge, restricted to a select few ... Because nearly everything that can be called neo-Pagan is eclectic, borrowing from several sources, there are overlaps between the various forms of neo-Paganism. There are links between some forms of Wicca and Druidry, and between both of these and Shamanism ...

From a 21st century standpoint, however, much of what now passes for pagan belief has jettisoned its former labels of 'occultism', 'witchcraft' and 'eccentricity', and now boasts a diverse doctrine, suitable for pre-pubescent schoolchildren to venerable pensioners, from all walks of life and cultures. On the traditionalist's side, this hard-won respectability means that, in many cases, both the genuine magical and Mystery aspects of the Old Ways have been abandoned in favour of a wholesome image more reminiscent of the fictitious 'Oxo family' than of the real-life Lancashire Witches.

It must be said from the onset that there is nothing wrong in anyone embracing a neo-pagan life-style. What we should try to do, however, is put into some kind of perspective the impact of the magico-religious links with our ancestral roots when we choose to follow a path or tradition that is alien to our own *genius loci* – **the collective or natural spirit of old Pretannia.** Whatever numerous contemporary authors may tell us, the Celts were *not* the indigenous people of these islands; modern Wicca is *not* synonymous with traditional witchcraft; traditional British Old Craft is *not* a myth; and subsequent invading cultures did *not* impose blanket religious conversions on a conquered people.

But what of the witchcraft, magic and Mysteries of what people today refer to as the Old Ways? They have existed for thousands of years, so can they really be so easily replaced in the Collective Unconscious? Is it true, as occult author Colin Wilson regularly maintains, that no one believes in magic any more? Is it too late to re-connect with the Old Ways?

The answer to those questions is, of course, a resounding; 'No! No! No!' – but we need to go back to our roots for the key. Or, more precisely, **to the roots of the path or tradition to which we feel instinctively drawn.** As the editor of *White Dragon* went on prophetically to observe, *the* real enemy of the Old Ways was never modern Christian (or even Islamic) fundamentalism, but the introduction of a contemporary eclectic, pick-and-mix approach that maintains that all universal god/desses are one, and that any permutation will do when it comes to supplication. At the advanced academic, theological, or higher ritual magic end of the spectrum this may be the case but at grass roots level, where most of us operate, it is essential to understand which deity (or force) represents a particular psychic energy ... when, where and why ... and how to tap into it.

In purely magical terms, Aphrodite is not compatible with Artemis and Athene; Isis does not equate with Diana or Freya – none of whom are indigenous goddesses to these islands. It is also important to accept that Names of Power do not represent *real* people, semi-divine or otherwise: this is a Christian concept that God is sitting there just waiting for our call. It is also detrimental to effective magical thinking. In magic, we use these mind-pictures, or correspondences, as a means of invoking (or evoking) the conceptualised power of individual energy-sources.

> ➤ In ancient times, the priesthood understood this – even if the common man did not.

In simple terms, imagine for a moment that we are faced by a huge bank of colour-coded electrical sockets, all having different strengths of electrical current running through them. These sockets represent the source of this elusive 'god-power'. In our hands we have a selection of colour-coded plugs representing the nature of the magical working we wish to undertake. If we make the wrong choice and connect, say, the red plug to a blue socket, it could result in:

- insufficient current coming through to power the magical working, or
- overload, in which case we blow a fuse and the whole working is either negated or incinerated.

This bank of sockets can also been seen as representing the Qabalistic Tree of Life, because each sphere (*sephirah*), is powered by different types of energy that are essentially both male and female, i.e. androgynous. To perform successful magical workings we must know *exactly* what we are plugging into before we start. In popularist teaching the goddess is All – and, as a result, the channelling of magical energies is knocked out of kilter, because in magical terms, Pan is *All* (*Pan Pangenetor*, the All-Begetter, represented by the 'Devil' in the Tarot). The experienced practitioner, however, isn't bothered about gender – he or she is bothered about getting on the right contacts and obtaining results. This is not denigrating anything; it is attempting to show that the modern witch or magical practitioner needs to think in purely abstract terms about magical energy and its application, not in religious or gender-specific ones.

Magic, of course, works best when there is a genuine magical partnership between god and goddess, man and woman. In certain kinds of rite, the woman knows that for it to be performed effectively, she remains passive/receptive, while her partner has the active/dynamic role. In other rituals it will necessitate the woman taking the active/dynamic role, while her partner remains passive/receptive. It's all a question of the energies being used in the correct manner for a particular ritual and nothing to do with gender superiority.

> ➤ **In ancient times, the priesthood understood this – even if the common man did not.**

Even if we work as solitary practitioners, we still need to understand that equilibrium is necessary to kick-start a magical operation – whether it be a simple healing charm, or a full-blown, bells and smells ritual. By mixing and mingling the energies of deities from different cultures, we negate not only their magical power, but also their spiritual influence, if we allow them to neutralise each other. And what many mistake for divine presence is merely an endorphin rush, caused by the transmission of chemical messages from the brain, which have the characteristic properties of opiate compounds such as morphine.

It has been medically acknowledged that there *is* a naturally occurring opiate in the human nervous system that can be induced by the clever use of music/rhythm/dance and language techniques. These naturally occurring endorphins produce the effect of 'spiritual mainlining' and those who experience the feel-good factor resulting from it are often convinced that deity has indeed touched them. The various priesthoods, pagan and otherwise, have been exploiting this reaction for years; while many solitary worshippers can induce it in themselves with repetitive chanting or dancing.

This, of course, explains where the 'Well, it works for me!' reasoning comes into the equation, that is so prevalent in many pagan responses, should they be criticised for their eclectic approach, or advised that a technique is wrong. Others claim to be expressing their own feelings in relation to their pagan belief, but perhaps we should ask ourselves, how can we express something unless we know what that something is, or if we haven't learned the basic canon for expressing it?

> In ancient times, the priesthood understood this – even if the common man did not.

Exploring Spirituality, co-written by myself and Aeron Medbh-Mara, pointed out that over the past few decades the focus of religion has moved from being of benefit to the group, to being the tool of the individual. Self-help psychology has played a large part in this shift, since it teaches that all the individual needs is within ourselves and, as a result, many of those following such 'experts' have subsequently become divorced from their *spiritual* roots. For practitioners of pagan ideologies, the thought processes are a little more insidious. Whereas the psychologist denies the existence of external deities, the modern pagan priesthood has a tendency to embrace the notion of every deity in existence, irrespective of its background, preference or allegiance.

What Exactly is Modern Paganism?

If we turn to contemporary publishing for the answer, we will find a veritable torrent of titles encompassing the 'mind, body and spirit' classification. Very little, however, offers up an erudite explanation for the here and now, about the cultural influences of the dim and distant past, without muddying the waters further downstream for the future. One publication defined the term paganism as 'nature worship that embraces the wider influences of other cultures, including Norse, Egyptian, Celtic, etc.,' in a form of 'eclectic paganism as it is increasingly becoming known'. Another popular release, jumping on the recent Tolkien-revival bandwagon, repeatedly talked about the Celts being the indigenous peoples of these isles – probably the same author who failed Michael Howard's (of *The Cauldron*) famous Celtic Potato test!

What You Call Time offered up a broad overview of how genuine Old Crafters saw themselves in terms of contemporary pagan labelling. What was immediately obvious was that even then (1998) the gulf between the various pagan, Wiccan and Craft traditions was immense, and many of these drastic changes had occurred within the previous three decades and for reasons we will discuss in a later chapter. Three traditional Old Craft witches gave their responses:

As a witch of long standing, I refuse to compromise my own integrity by pandering to the current demand for the politically correct, neo-paganism that is now passing itself off as Craft. It's time people understood that Craft isn't for everyone.

It's about harnessing the natural energies in a time-honoured way. This is our way of life, it's being going on for centuries and we know the magic works. We have no intention of changing our ways and would rather go into the shadows than compromise.

We will continue to refuse 'initiation on demand' in order to satisfy the 'gimme, gimme' mentality of the modern generation of would-be witches, who seem to think it their right to claim kinship on the grounds that it is now fashionable to be labelled a Wiccan or pagan.

Unfortunately, a great deal of modern pagan worship *is* an eclectic cross-pollination of different cultures, which means that contemporary British paganism is indeed shot through with Celtic, Druidic, Roman, Anglo-Saxon and Norse influences, not forgetting a frequent Roman, Greek, Egyptian and Oriental overlay. 'Which is not conducive to successful magic,' added another witch. 'It might appear to be a broad-based view of religious thinking but from the magical perspective, it is completely self-defeating.'

We can see that things have evolved a long way from the primal applications of traditional Old Craft, through the highly formalised rituals of the Gardnerian and Alexandrian traditions, to emerge as the informal, eco-pagan worship of modern Wicca. In fact, a large majority of pagans are adamant that they do not practice any form of magic despite buying thousands of books on charms and spellcasting for the purpose of attracting a mate, divination, crystal lore, gaining wealth and healing. A growing number admit to not knowing the name of Gerald Gardner, the 'Founding Father' of the belief they profess to follow, and tantamount to a self-proclaimed Christian not knowing who Jesus was! They make their claims on the grounds that the focus of their devotion is centred on the goddess/mother figure and that this way is open to all; even though a large number of the rituals given in popular books on the subject are thinly disguised ritual magic and Freemasonry served up as goddess worship.

Fortunately there are always those whose curiosity prompts them to dig deeper and discover the true Old Ways – but this is not always as easy as they would wish. Magical tutors are often confronted by the situation whereby if the student has not been admitted to the Inner Secrets of the Cosmos by Lesson Four, they become disgruntled. Then, taking what little information they have managed to ingest, they go off to start a group of their own, thereby perpetuating the watering down of Craft-lore every time there is a division of interest. Magical development can be likened to learning a new language. We may have a smattering of well-known phrases and colloquialisms at guidebook level, but if we wish to become fluent speakers, then we need to go back to basics to learn the lesser mysteries of grammar and syntax.

As experienced magical practitioners know, these Lesser Mysteries are in themselves merely the next level of basic teachings that are available to all, whether in book form or by elementary tuition. What many choose to ignore is the existence of the Greater Mysteries, which can only be understood through personal quest and experience: they cannot be taught in words. As Alan Richardson points out in his *Introduction to the Mystical Qabalah*, 'Books and teachers can only give a few inadequate methods to reach the wisdom that is nowhere else but within the seeker. That is why it is a pointless exercise searching through books for any Universal Secret. It does not exist.'

This is not, of course, what would-be seekers wish to hear, despite the fact that this is the only explanation any genuine tradition or teacher can possibly give. It is probably a bitter pill to swallow, as we have all, in our time, assembled an impressive working knowledge of other people's rituals and correspondences – but for what purpose? The more we learn, the more we expect to be the recipients of higher or advanced information in order to progress magically or mystically. But to go back to Alan Richardson: 'The rest is up to us, for there is no dogma, no secret teachings, no mysterious Adepts, nor anything which can help us avoid doing a great deal of work ...'

Neither should the seeker be fooled by a tradition that claims to trace its antecedents back to medieval or even pre-historic times. Even archaeologists and historians cannot provide information as to how the paths to these ancient Mysteries were structured, so it is pointless for a 20th century revivalist organisation to claim that it does! In all reality, the tracing of any genuine Old Craft coven back more than 150 years is a challenge in itself. That said it is **still possible to honour the gods as they were honoured** *within their own time and place* **within Britain's long history of religious and cultural development.**

The actual spiritual beliefs of our Mesolithic ancestors are so far removed in time from contemporary society that it is impossible to say with any certainty what the real meaning is in the clues they have left behind. It is possible that the Druids of the Iron Age *may* have preserved earlier knowledge as part of their complex oral tradition, which was handed down from generation to generation, but this is by no means a certainty. Like later beliefs, these threads would have been tenuous and, to the invaders, the gods of the earlier peoples would probably have been degraded or 'demonised' in later Anglo-Saxon folklore.

Mountainous regions, however, remained largely isolated from social change and particularly the upheavals in the lowland south that followed the collapse of the Roman Empire. As a result, the oral traditions of these predominantly static populations were more likely to preserve older beliefs, many of which have survived to the present day as folklore. By rule of thumb, it is probably accurate to say that the local spirits or entities feared or loathed by one race, were sacred to the people they had deposed.

The first acceptance is learning to judge any ancient culture by its own lights, not by those of our generation; the second is understanding where to draw the line of demarcation between the differing waves of cultural invaders. Thirdly, we need to be aware that for our ancient ancestors, wherever they came from, magic and the Mysteries were synonymous with the religion of the people of that time. The two became separated as the

Christian church became more established and native beliefs were either suppressed, merged into the church calendar, or 'went into the shadows'. For the vast majority of modern pagans, this ancient rift between the two remains unhealed.

Nevertheless, C G Jung maintained that the human mind had been shaped and affected by hundreds of thousands of years of all this human experience, and that a concentrated essence of what is commonly referred to by occultists as the *Anima Mundi* (the world soul), is buried deep within the minds of each of us. Magical teaching is based on a vast variety of techniques, which enable the seeker to use one, or many, of the various astral doorways to reconnect with the *Anima Mundi* for the purpose of mystical or divinatory exploration.

It is this reconnection with the Collective Unconscious that re-establishes our root-memory with the past, not some tenuous belief in reincarnation or past-life regression. What we also know is that the Mysteries are common to all beliefs and traditions, regardless of time and place. The Mysteries are based on Truth, and Truth is Truth; the Truth of yesterday is the Truth of tomorrow. The quest of any seeker should be based on curiosity and the desire to find that Truth – which can only be achieved by studying our own ancestral history – once the seeker knows *how* to look.

Chapter Two

A Haunted Landscape (Pre-history)

It is my contention that the influences of British pre-Roman cultures are still of fundamental importance to modern British society ... The six millennia of insular development gave British culture a unique identity and strength that was able to survive the tribulations posed by the Roman Conquest, and the folk movements of the post-Roman Migration Period, culminating in the Danish raids, the Danelaw and of course the Norman Conquest of 1066.
Francis Pryor, *Britain BC*

There is a self-perpetuating myth that has clouded the view we have of our distant ancestors. All too often they are seen as 'noble savages', primitive, barbaric people with few 'civilised' attributes, until the Romans came along. Archaeologist Francis Pryor dismisses all that. According to *his* research, all the Romans can take credit for was wiping out a 10,000-year old island culture quite unlike any other in the ancient world. Pryor also maintains that from as early as the Late Stone Age, Britain had evolved into a highly sophisticated farming culture, which could comfortably support its small tribes or groups.

What *we* are looking for, however, is historical evidence of any *religious* observances because, as every student of magic knows, religion and magic have been inextricably entwined ever since those dim and distant times. And what is also a recognised fact is that all beliefs, past and present, have something to say about death as a precursor to established religion. As Pascal Boyer points out in *Religion Explained*, the connection between notions of supernatural agents and representations about death may take different forms in different human groups, but there is always some connection. 'Why is that so? One straightforward answer is that our concepts and emotions about death are quite simply the origin of religious concept.'

Our Stone Age ancestors' beliefs probably grew from a very natural human need to explain puzzling natural phenomena, and in no time at all, the existence and – as Boyer refers to them – 'causal powers of non-observable entities and agencies' would have become an established part of tribal psychology. As a result, the death of a tribal member would therefore be marked with ritual customs, for no people, no matter how primitive, were going to take pains to engage in even the most rudimentary of funerary preparations if they did not hold some belief in the continuance of a 'spirit form' after the extinction of physical life.

As fascinating as British pre-history is, we must focus solely on the religious aspects in order to attempt to reconstruct some of those ancestral customs that we can identify with today's contemporary beliefs. According to archaeologists Francis Pryor and Barry Cunliffe, there is a great deal of evidence to show that European and Middle Eastern Neanderthals cared deeply about death and their dead: burials were deliberately placed in 'graves', and bodies sometimes accompanied by grave goods were painted with red ochre – a natural powder-based mineral. So even at this very early stage of human evolution, there is convincing evidence of some form of belief in an afterlife, or careful interment of the bodies would not have been deemed necessary.

One of the most significant finds in Britain was the discovery of the Cro-Magnon skeleton of the Red Lady of Paviland Cave on the Gower Peninsula, which dates from the Early Palaeolithic period, some 3,000 years *before* the end of the last Ice Age. First discovered in 1822, the skeleton was thought to be that of a woman, but modern re-examination reveals it to be that of a young man aged 25 to 30.

The grave goods included a mammoth ivory bracelet and a perforated periwinkle pendant, numerous seashells and some 50 broken ivory rods. Marker stones were placed at the head and foot of the grave, although the skull was missing. The red ochre still colours the ornaments and bones, although there is a variance between the colour of the bones of the arms and chest, and the hips and legs. Archaeologists have suggested that he was buried in a two-piece garment; the feet being only slightly stained, which indicates that he may have worn shoes.

The DNA extracted from the bones can be related to the commonest ancestry extant in Europe, and strongly suggests that many of our forebears were already inhabiting these islands in the Palaeolithic period, rather than arriving with the Neolithic farmers who introduced the concept of farming just prior to Britain's separation from mainland Europe. Radio-carbon dating also revealed that some of the artefacts were 'slightly later' than the Red Lad's original burial, indicating that the cave was used repeatedly over a period of some 4,000 years.

Paviland, or Goat's Hole Cave, is located at what was the extreme northern edge of the Early Upper Palaeolithic world, when the climate was teetering on the brink of another Ice Age. Standing at the water margin and looking towards the cave, Francis Pryor observed that it was comparable with other important places in 'the religion and mythological lives of people with shamanistic religions'.

Without stretching credulity too far, we can surmise that Paviland was a sacred site, and that the Red Lad's burial confirms a significant belief in an afterlife; possibly a form of ancestor worship as is suggested in the careful preservation of the body, and the placement of later offerings. This obviously 'holy man' belonged to the first or earlier part of the Upper Palaeolithic period – just prior to the onset of the last Ice Age some 25,000 years ago. During its coldest phase (approximately 18,000 years ago) most of northern Europe, including the area that was later to become the British Isles, was uninhabited – effectively sealing the Red Lad in an ice tomb.

About 13,000 years ago, when our quest really begins, the ice and cold receded, and the plants and animals upon which man subsisted began to re-establish themselves. Humans followed in their wake, and although the landscape was a treeless steppe, it is here that we must begin ... by putting our pre-history into some sort of perspective.

Five Ages of Prehistoric Britain

Palaeolithic (before 8000BC): Man lived by hunting, fishing and food gathering (e.g. nuts, roots and berries), often dwelling in caves in the winter but migratory during the summer months, following the herds of reindeer and horse upon which they depended. Much evidence was destroyed by the Ice Age but many animals, such as mammoth, wild horse, reindeer, bison, woolly rhino and hyena, quickly became extinct in the British Isles. There is no firm evidence of any settlement in Ireland.

Mesolithic (8000 to 3250BC): Man still practised a shifting hunter-gatherer culture, not strictly nomadic but without permanent settlements. There is increasing evidence of human habitation in northern England, Scotland and Ireland. Around 6000BC the land-bridge linking Britain with the continent was broken and Britain became an island. The landscape was now predominantly woodland and scrub, which led to the decline of the reindeer and horse herds. The first evidence of temporary woodland clearances has been found in areas of Dartmoor and the Cleveland Hills, and by the end of the Mesolithic era there was an identifiable colonisation across Britain, including one of the more important sites in England: Star Carr (North Yorkshire), which was set against the pre-6000BC shoreline.

Neolithic (3250 to 1700BC): Forest clearances became more widespread as man began to farm the land to produce grain crops. Settlements were generally on high ground where many longbarrow burial chambers can still be found; and there is evidence of an extensive trade in stone axes around Britain. Early embanked sanctuaries or 'henges' were built, sometimes with stone, although these were mostly of a later period.

Bronze Age (1700 to 500BC): Metallurgical skills developed sufficiently to make bronze weapons and ornamental objects, but stone and wooden implements (including a primitive plough in the late Bronze Age) were still used in agriculture. More forest clearing is evident and stone circles tend to date from this period, as do round barrows (tumuli) and cairns. Ireland's gold brought new settlers and trade, not only with Britain but also with continental Europe; there is increasing evidence of lowland settlements, notably in the English Midlands.

Iron Age (500BC to 43AD): Many hilltop settlements were developed into hill-forts, often defended by vast ramparts and serving as tribal capitals. Settlement patterns become more varied with farmsteads and small villages or hamlets as well as the larger communities associated with the biggest hill-forts. Cattle and sheep grazing became more common and trade routes expanded. Much of Scotland and Ireland remained in the Bronze Age for several centuries, but may have entered the Iron Age with the builders of hill-forts, possibly about 200BC. Many facets of Iron Age and Celtic society survived the Roman occupation, particularly in highland Scotland and Ireland, which were largely or totally unaffected by Roman influence.

[All dates are approximate and there were often important regional variations from the generalised summaries above.]

Late Upper Palaeolithic

Another significant find from the Late Upper Palaeolithic period was the discovery at Gough's Cave in Cheddar Gorge. First excavated in the 1890s and again, more fully, in the 1980s when the remains of at least three adults and two children, one aged from 11 to 13, and the other three to five years. Unlike the Red Lad at Paviland, these bodies were not deliberately arranged but loose, disarticulated bones jumbled among flint tools, pieces of antler, bone and mammoth ivory.

Under the microscope, the human bones showed extensive scratches that suggested that the corpses had been carefully dismembered. Francis Pryor (*Britain BC*) believes that this was 'something ceremonial, symbolic and special'. It could have been an act of hostility to a vanquished foe but, he suggests, it was more likely to have been an act of respect to a departed relative. We know from later evidence that later peoples practised a form of multi-stage burial and cremation, and it is possible that the remains at Gough's Cave are a form of interment similar to those found in purpose-built communal tombs. Pryor suggests that the meticulous dismemberment of the bodies gives the impression that the detached portions were placed in a special area reserved for bodies or souls that were still in a transitional state, or part of a two-stage funerary process.

Among the many items found at Gough's Cave were pieces of Baltic amber – and it is important to note that this was valued as far back as the Upper Palaeolithic and Mesolithic times. Later in pre-history, particularly in the Early Bronze Age (around 2000BC), it was widely traded and made into some extraordinarily beautiful objects, including a large variety of beads and elaborate multi-stranded necklaces. So we know for certain that both amber and ivory were used as possible protective objects (amulets) from the earliest point in our history.

Mesolithic or New Stone Age

Moving into the Mesolithic, or New Stone Age, the next important find was that of Star Carr, situated in the Vale of Pickering in Yorkshire. The site was discovered during the cleaning of a field drain and excavation began in 1949, continuing until 1951; radio-carbon dating of the remains suggesting a date c7500BC. Star Carr affirms the highly developed hunting prowess of our ancestors but, more importantly, it produced a wealth of information about hunting techniques and revealed the first use of dogs in support of the chase.

In *Late Stone Age Hunters of the British Isles,* Christopher Smith points out that although Mesolithic people may well have gathered plants for food to supplement their mainly meat-based diet, they were always far more hunters than gatherers. Although Star Carr was a hunting camp rather than a settlement, there were some amazing finds that support the theory that each group or tribe followed some form of shamanic ritual belief. Among the remains were 21 red deer skull fragments, known as frontlets, some complete with antlers that had been cut down 'in such as way as to still look impressive, and more or less balanced, but not to be so heavy'.

The underside of these frontlets had the sharp ridges knocked away, and were perforated with two or four circular holes. Archaeologists have suggested that these were head-dresses that could be secured by hide straps through the holes, and used in ceremonial dances, possibly reminiscent of the Abbots Bromley Horn Dance ... and/or used as a disguise when out stalking. Christopher Smith argues in favour of the latter, reasoning that being a hunting-camp, the frontlets must have had a practical use. **Sympathetic magic *is* practical, and similar depictions can be found in cave-paintings all over the world.**

As well as being meat-eaters, our Mesolithic ancestors also included a wide variety of other foods in their diet. Various excavations have shown that, depending on the season and location, they enjoyed a varied diet of salmon, cod and sea trout, eel, wild pig, venison, game and sea birds, cockles, hazelnuts ... all identified from the rubbish left behind in their camps. Bristol University researchers have also discovered evidence that milk and cheese were part of the staple diet 6,000 years ago, having found milk fat on cooking vessels used around 4000BC. These would have also been the foods offered up as part of ritual observance in a dominantly hunter-gatherer society.

A burial site in the Mendip Hills, although first discovered in 1793, has only recently been accurately dated, with some startling results. The cave, where Stone Age hunters laid their dead to rest more than 10,000 years ago, has now been acknowledged as the oldest cemetery in Britain. Radio-carbon dating showed that the bodies were interred in the cave, known as Aveline's Hole, between 10,200 and 10,400 years ago – a few centuries after the last Ice Age, and 4,000 years earlier than previously thought.

Two boys chasing a rabbit into a hole originally discovered the bodies: around 100 skeletons lying side by side, which were subsequently excavated and stored. Ironically, all but 21 were destroyed in a German bombing raid on Bristol in 1940. The surviving bones, having now been analysed, also revealed clues about the diet and habits of the people of the Mesolithic period. The dead, including slightly-built adults of around five foot tall and several children, all died relatively young. Some teeth showed repeated periods of poor nutrition or chronic childhood illness, with signs of iron deficiency and little evidence of fish in the diet. The find has also challenged the long-held view that our hunter-gatherer ancestors were totally nomadic, and suggests that some had a very positive sense of 'territory' and 'ancestors'.

In Britain, construction of the large stone monuments has traditionally been attributed to the arrival of the Neolithic people, but according to Francis Pryor's *Britain BC*, a few hints are beginning to emerge that it was never quite as straightforward as that.

Neolithic

By 4500BC, farming communities had begun to spring up over wide areas of Britain and some 'system of calendrical notation had to be called into being to enable the events of the farming cycle to be sited appropriately in time' (*The Calendar*). In other words, those who were settling down on the land needed to be able to calculate and predict the 'wheel of the year', and this would have been achieved in exactly the same way as every other ancient civilisation – by charting the cycles of the sun, moon and stars.

The Peak District probably sports the finest collection of temples and tombs left by those who first made their homes in the fertile limestone valleys. The great henge and stone circle at Arbor Low, near Monyash, is probably the most famous sacred megalithic site in England after Stonehenge and Avebury. Today, all but one of the stones has fallen and yet Arbor Low remains an impressive place to visit, with its panoramic views looking out over hill and moorland. The henge itself is the best known ancient site in the Peak District, but the area is also rich with monuments constructed during the Neolithic and Bronze Ages, including remains of chambered tombs, stone circles and the burial mounds, or 'lows' from the Old English word *hlaw*. Like other monuments of the time, archaeologists believe that the layout of the stones were aligned to mark sunrises and sunsets, and the cycles of the moon and stars, on which those primitive calendar reckonings would have been based.

What we must keep reminding ourselves, however, is to avoid applying the 'noble savage' principle as if those remote beings lived in some idyllic Golden Age. Civilisation has always progressed in fits and starts and, although there is no evidence to support the idea, it is obvious that highly distinctive social groupings would have been developing over a very long period of time. Disputes over territorial possession and hereditary would have been inevitable, and in the light of the colossal and widespread constructions of the Neolithic era, there must have been some powerful 'chiefs' around to channel the energy of thousands of 'indians' into constructing those massive monuments at Avebury, Arbor Low, Silbury Hill and Stonehenge.

What would also be developing alongside all this social settling, were the religious beliefs of the people and the 'astronomer-priests' of the time would have needed a very convincing line in argument for the 'construction of monuments of such grandiose conception and execution'. In *The Historical Atlas of Britain*, Nigel Saul observes that it has been calculated that Silbury Hill would have required nine million man-hours for its construction, and the principal phase of Stonehenge more than thirty million. Needless to say, we have no means of knowing how long these projects actually took, but as Nigel Saul points out, they are inconceivable without very large numbers of people being organised, controlled and supplied for long periods of time. 'This suggests strongly the concentration of power into relatively few hands within each region of the country ...'

As we can see, it would be a mistake to believe that this social development of the British peoples blossomed from Mesolithic hunter-gatherers to fully-fledged, Neolithic monument builders overnight, with a conveniently datable cut-off point. All of these transformations took place over an extended period of time, but as Francis Pryor observes: 'To my mind both were the same Stone Age people whose roots lay back in the Upper Palaeolithic, at sites like Paviland and Gough's Cave.' It is therefore not unreasonable to suggest that, just like the religion of ancient Egypt, the beliefs of the ancient Britons had evolved from tribal shamanism to a highly sophisticated and powerful astronomer-priesthood as a natural progression; the tribal shaman (witch/healer) possibly being sidelined into the remoter areas of Britain where his/her influence would have retained its mystery away from the developing lowland community astronomer-priesthood.

For confirmation along this line of thinking, we now turn to the views of leading British astrophysicist and cosmologist, Sir (then Professor) Fred Hoyle, who said of Stonehenge: 'It seemed obvious that whoever had constructed this structure had been impelled by much the same motives as the builders of medieval cathedrals.' Whatever the wonder of the astronomical uses for the site, it is impossible to ignore the compelling religious motivation behind the building of monuments of this magnitude.

Hoyle became involved in the astronomical debate over Stonehenge, which was raging between Gerald Hawkins, author of *Stonehenge Decoded*, and 'respectable archaeological opinion of the time'; the latter enlisting the eminent astronomer's help in refuting Hawkins' claims that Stonehenge was an astronomical observatory. No doubt much to the chagrin of his detractors and by using precise mathematical formulae for the movement of the moon, and the sun at the solstices, he wrote, '...within quite trivial margins, I confirmed all of Hawkins' results'.

Stonehenge, as we know it today, developed and evolved over a very long period of time; its construction spans an enormous period – from about 3000BC-1000BC. This impressive monument is probably the best indication of how the magico-religious beliefs of the people grew in importance, because only something that is so deeply rooted in 'faith' can produce such sustained efforts from a willing people.

- **Stonehenge I:** The first construction was a ditch and bank, in the form of a circle some 300 feet in diameter with a single entrance to the north-east, which dates from around 3,000BC. Outside the entrance stood an unworked block of sarsen stone weighing some 25 tons, known today as the Heel Stone.
- **Stonehenge II:** This second stage consisted of positioned stones outside what was to become the main structure. The entrance to the ditched enclosure was widened in order to be accurately aligned with the contemporary midsummer sunrise/midwinter sunset. An avenue of two parallel ditches was laid out to the north-east and the River Avon, and four 'station stones' of unworked sarsen stone were

set at four points just within the bank of the enclosure.

• **Stonehenge III:** The bluestones for this central part were brought from the Prescelli Mountains in Wales, some 320 kilometres away, around 2200BC. There is also evidence that the pillars and lintels of volcanic tufa, myolite and spotted dolerite had been used in another monument before their appearance on the site at Stonehenge. Shortly before 2000BC a total of 74 great sarsen blocks were imported to the site, probably from Marlborough Down.

What is rarely mentioned, probably because the actual site is now covered by the present-day car park, is the discovery of four post-holes that had been dug to contain pine posts some two to three feet in diameter, and which simply had to have had some ritual or religious function. What makes this find so remarkable is the range of radio-carbon dating and pollen analysis spanning between 8500BC and 7650BC, which proves that early Stonehenge and its immense landscape of ritual barrows and other sites, was positioned within a **sacred area that was already 4,000 years old when the first Neolithic people appeared on the scene.**

In later ages, the focus of the site may have changed considerably – possibly even subjected to deliberate acts of desecration. Michael Howard, author of *The Sacred Earth Guide*, wrote for *Alphard* magazine that archaeologists had pronounced Stonehenge to be Britain's psychic Chernobyl, which had been the site of public executions during the first millennia of the Christian era. New forensic examination of four skeletons, unearthed at the henge in 1923, revealed that one was of a man who had been beheaded using an iron sword, the angle of the cut suggesting that the victim might have been kneeling with his back towards his killer.

Previous archaeological speculation had suggested that Stonehenge had become overgrown and neglected by the time the Romans arrived in Britain, but new discoveries indicate that it was in use for a far longer period. Apart from the exhumations in the 1920s, three other skeletons have since been found on the site: two dating from the Stone Age, one of whom had died in a hail of flint-tipped arrows. The other was a male from the Roman period. Howard wrote:

The old name for Stonehenge is 'stone gallows' and as far as I am concerned this name and the recent findings both fit the circle perfectly. When I first visited it in the 1960s, my impression was of a dark atmosphere of blood sacrifice, violence and death. Subsequent events in the last twenty years at the stones have only confirmed my initial feeling that it is a place that attracts negative energy. It has to be accepted that not all ancient sites possess a positive, life-affirming energy, have a good atmosphere, or a beneficial effect on visitors just because they were, or are, sacred centres for (ancient) religious worship.

By 2750BC, work had also begun on Silbury Hill, the largest man-made mound in Europe, which may have taken well over 100 years to complete. On completion, it was a stepped chalk structure, shining white and built to an incredible height of 40 metres; its original function is unknown but its completion may have marked the beginning of the construction of the Avebury monument. While in the north, the unique triple henge at Thornborough, one of Britain's largest ritual enclosures, was constructed. Each henge is 240 metres in diameter, while the whole complex is over a mile in length. There has been a suggestion that the three henges were aligned with the stars in Orion's belt as they appear in the sky around the Winter Solstice.

On a much more practical level, excavation of the Sweet Track, a linear causeway running for nearly two kilometres across the Somerset fens, revealed some extremely interesting discoveries. From around 4000BC, the area now known as the Somerset Levels was becoming increasingly wetter and in the winter of 3807BC-6BC a plank walkway of oak, hazel and alder was laid across the marsh. Alongside the trackway, concealed in the peat, the excavators found an unused flint axe and an axe of jadeite (its source identified as the foothills of the Alps), fine pottery bowls, wooden pins, wooden bowls, a pot of hazelnuts and leaf arrowheads – objects that might suggest votive offerings rather than carelessness.

These finds from the Sweet Track give us the first example of a pre-Celtic tradition of making offerings 'at the water's edge', and the rare jadeite axe would have been a very costly gift. They also demonstrate that Britain was no longer as insular as we might have previously thought, with evidence of trade from the continent beginning to become more and more apparent.

Excavations of buildings of the period (radio-carbon dated to around 3310BC-2910BC), also revealed a very special kind of construction – a house for the remains of the dead. One discovery was a beautiful, shiny jet pendant, and a fragment from a green-coloured, volcanic tuff axe, rock that occurs at Langdale, in the Lake District, some 175 miles north of the site. This Fengate house formed part of a row of structures that were all about death and the afterlife, one of which contained a multiple burial of a Neolithic man, woman and their two children.

Our Neolithic ancestors would not have drawn any distinction between the spiritual or temporal; for them ancestral spirits and supernatural forces would be directly influencing daily life. Care would have to be taken not to incur the wrath of those ancestors whose spirits resided in barrows and hidden, solitary graves, since these spirits were capable of inflicting all manner of unpleasantness on the living. 'The landscape in which these people lived was real, but it was also in part a landscape of the mind: hills, trees, rivers and manmade monuments such as barrows had their own tales to tell,' observes Francis Pryor. Here we have mythology and supernatural forces forming more than just a backdrop to people's daily lives. Everything interleaved and intertwined, binding the landscape and the spirit world together.

Bronze Age

Many graves dating to two or three centuries before 2000BC contain a variety of beautifully worked grave goods and the highly decorated drinking vessels known as 'beakers'. This distinctive style of pottery has been found across most of Europe, and is often associated with the first appearance of metal-working. This also indicates that there was a lot more movement between the peoples of Europe, as Barry Cunliffe observes in *Facing the Ocean*. He suggests that the greatest change to come about during this period was the gradual abandonment of long-established collective burials in megalithic monuments, replaced by a custom of single body burial. The deceased was now treated as an individual as signified by separate burial, together with provision of funerary equipment appropriate to the status in life.

Archaeological findings suggest that this custom may have originated in northern Europe around 3000BC and spread rapidly over most of central and western Europe by 2300BC. The new style of interment usually included a pottery beaker, with graves of the period giving up barbed and tanged arrowheads, a perforated stone wrist-guard, a tanged copper dagger and stone battleaxes. The marked similarity between the findings gave rise to the term 'Beaker People' and there was a great deal of specu-lation as to where these migrants might have come from. New scientific data, however, suggests that this 'Beaker package' was adopted within a very short space of time by the indigenous communities throughout western Europe. Barry Cunliffe offers the explanation that the burial customs of neighbouring societies might be perceived to be more attractive because of their exotic nature, and may have been adopted by the emerging elite in order to distinguish themselves from those of lower status in their own society.

The richest early Bronze Age burial (c.2300BC) found in Britain to date, is that of a mature man found near Amesbury about three miles from Stonehenge, which contained far more grave goods than any other burial of this period. A spokesman for Wessex Archaeology pointed out that although the area is rich in Bronze Age burials, this particular find is several hundred years earlier than any of them, and unique in the quality and quantity of the grave goods. The man has been identified as an archer on the basis of the stone arrowheads and stone wrist-guards that protected the arm from the recoil of the bow. There were also stone toolkits for butchering carcasses, and for making arrowheads.

As well as archery equipment, the man had three copper knives and a pair of gold earrings, which appear to have been wrapped around the ear, rather than hanging from the lobe. These are some of the earliest metal objects found in Britain, and may have been imported. The fact that so many valuable objects have been found together *is* unique, and the most important thing about the find is the question of *who* this archer was, and why his mourners buried so many valuables with him.

The Archer, who was five feet nine inches tall, lacked a left knee-cap, suggesting a serious injury. He was aged between 35 and 50 when he died and was placed in a timber chamber. Further tests, however, showed some surprising results. According to archaeologists, tests on the teeth of the Amesbury Archer revealed that he had probably travelled from the Alps, and support the theory that an extensive European trade network existed in the early Bronze Age. The gold hair tresses in his grave (which date to c2470BC) are the earliest gold objects found in Britain and suggest that he may have imported metalworking skills, which would have given him great status. Because he lived at the same time that the inner circle of bluestones of Stonehenge were being erected and was buried close by, archaeologists suggest that he may have been involved in its creation.

Andrew Fitzpatrick of Wessex Archaeology explained that it really was a time of great change in Britain, when the skills of metalworking were being brought here from abroad. Historians have long suspected that it was continental visitors who initiated the trade that first brought metalworking to Britain, and the Archer is the first discovery to confirm this. Tests carried out on the Archer's teeth and bones, and on objects in the grave, including the gold hair tresses, three copper knives and five pots, revealed that the knives came from Spain and France, while the oxygen isotopes in his teeth suggest he came from an Alpine region, probably Switzerland. Another skeleton from the same period has since been found only five yards away. These remains were those of a man, aged 25-30, buried in the same posture, on his left side with his face to the north and legs bent, but in this case his grave was bare, except for the sharpened tusk of a boar and basket-shaped gold ear-rings.

Excavations have also unearthed one of the oldest treasures ever to be found in Britain: a gold ceremonial cup fashioned by Bronze Age artisans. Four and a half inches high and weighing 100g, the cup was beaten out of a solid lump of 20-carat gold, embossed and buried in a round barrow close to the grave of an important chieftain from around 1600BC. This new find, named the Ringlemere Cup, was excavated in a round barrow, around 100 feet across and encircled by a six-feet-deep ditch. A grave pit was found at the centre of the barrow, close to where the cup was buried, although no skeleton has come to light – possibly because the surrounding soil is so acidic. Stone Age flints and pottery have also been found, suggesting that the site was occupied since at least 5000BC.

But it wasn't just a change in Bronze Age burial rites that have astounded the scientists. A skull discovered on the banks of the Thames may have belonged to one of the first Londoners to undergo a form of trepanation. Radio-carbon dating has placed the skull between 1750BC and 1610BC (Middle Bronze Age), and bone re-growth shows that the patient survived this drastic treatment, which was unusual, said Dr Simon Mays of English Heritage. 'Nor is there evidence of post-operative infection, a leading cause of death. He would have been walking around happily with this hole in his head for a long period.'

This suggests anatomical and surgical skills were also in evidence and not bettered in Europe until classical Greek and Roman times **more than a thousand years later**. In fact, about 40 trepanned skulls are known in Britain, with the oldest dating back another 1,000 years to the Neolithic period. The ancients thought trepanation could cure headaches; some believed that evil spirits causing epilepsy or mental illness could escape through a hole in the skull.

This widespread movement of people, knowledge and goods for trade, continually endorses the belief that our Bronze Age ancestors were a lot more advanced than we have previously given them credit for. They may also have been a lot wealthier. The mysterious 'lines' discovered in aerial photographs taken in the 1950s, which baffled archaeologists for years, have now been identified as cattle runs along which thousands of cattle were moved between settlements and watering holes. English Heritage commented that we are looking at the remains of a highly sophisticated cattle business more reminiscent of *High Chaparral* than small-scale peasant farming. The remains of a vast Bronze Age cattle-ranch were also discovered across eight miles of the Yorkshire Wolds, running across the chalk hills near the village of Weaverthorpe, together with evidence of large scale farming. This also may go a long way to explain how these so-called 'primitive' societies could afford to sacrifice such large numbers of animals in their celebratory rites and ritual observances.

And yet some things did not change. The finds around the Fiskerton timber causeway echo the earlier offerings found at

Sweet Track, where ordinary people cast a wide range of items into the waters as if in homage to some indigenous water god. Wide expanses of water were often believed to be the spiritual resting places of the dead, and although earlier people had put a tremendous amount of effort into the construction of ritual and ceremonial centres related to their ancestors, from the middle of the Bronze Age these vast monuments were no longer maintained. Instead, increasing emphasis appears to have been placed on the ritual importance of rivers and watery places. David Miles informs us in *The Tribes of Britain* that valuable objects were not only found in the Thames, but also in rivers such as the Witham, the Shannon and in the margins of the Fens.

The timbers at Fiskerton also provided some astounding insights into the sophistication of the late Bronze Age/Early Iron Age communities, which echo the wisdom of the astronomer-priesthood of earlier times. The various rebuilds to the causeway, when new timbers were inserted, closely coincided with total lunar eclipses. The earliest was in the winter of 457/6BC; the next rebuilding took place ten years later, in the winter/spring of 447BC. Several subsequent episodes of reconstruction also coincided with total lunar eclipses. These preliminary results suggest that as some of the eclipses would not have been visible from the actual site: the rebuilding work **did not follow the eclipses, they predicted them**. And since this is not a simple business – they follow a cycle known as 'saros', of 18 years, 10 days – the findings further endorse the astronomical capabilities of our prehistoric ancestors.

Iron Age

The Iron Age was the shortest period of British prehistory, but it witnessed some remarkable social changes: the introduction of the hierarchical system, the emergence of the warrior leaders who built the massive hill forts, and the arrival of a large number of migrants, who brought their own cultures with them.

During this time, the central part of England was dominated by the forts, usually positioned on prominent or commanding hilltops and often visible for miles around. They were fortified by one or more ditches, which were supported by a steep bank, or rampart, on the inside. The original fortifications were built up with massive timber stockades and walls, designed to deter an attack. These forts were also places where large numbers of people could come together for religious purposes, for social-ising, or trade, as well as defence. Danebury (Hampshire) was first occupied around 550BC and came to an abrupt end around 100BC, when the main fortified gate was burnt to the ground. There is little archaeological evidence to suggest that any pitched battles were fought at the site, and the skirmishes that led to the slain and mutilated bodies found in the locality were more likely to be a result of tribal feuding rather than full-scale warfare.

Archaeologists have recently found the remains of an Iron Age nobleman, buried in his chariot, which gives a valuable insight into the customs and social standing of a member of the Parisii tribe. Carbon dating suggests the burial took place between 400BC-500BC with evidence of a large feast. Chariot burials were reserved for people of high rank and only a handful of such graves have been discovered; the latest find being only the second where the chariot was buried intact. The bones of the owner, whose age has been determined at between 30 and 40, and the metal 'tyres' of the three-foot spoked wheels remained intact in a limestone cavity. The wood had rotted away, leaving stains and hollows that outlined its shape. Iron and bronze harness fittings were recovered as well as grave goods, including an iron spearhead and the bones of pork joints – probably offerings to the gods. Thousands of cattle bones from the feast suggested it was for a person of great power who was revered by a large number of people.

The horse has, of course, a deep and revered place in the British psyche. The White Horse at Uffington was cut into the side of the hill where three tribal territories met and is the first 'uniquely British art in our history'. In *The Seven Ages of Britain*, Justin Pollard observes that it was not a new feature of the landscape in the Iron Age. In fact, archaeological research has shown that a thousand years might already have passed since Bronze Age farmers had cut deep trenches into the hillside in the shape of a horse before they began the laborious task of removing white chalk from another hill (the bedrock on Uffington Hill was not white enough), and carrying it in baskets to pack into the trenches. 'A millennium later this figure still stood out on the hillside, still retained its meaning, and might have gained more over the centuries.'

The actual religious beliefs of the people appear to have changed little. Water and wet places still played an important part in Iron Age religion, according to *Britain BC*, and there can be little doubt that the roots of these water-based rituals lay in the Bronze Age, or even earlier – although the rites that attended these ceremonies became distinctively modified from one region to another. 'If offerings placed in pits harked back to earlier practices, the placing of metal objects in the Thames continued unabated.'

Perhaps it was this affinity with water that led the Iron Age people to construct yet another remarkable feat of engineering. Scientists believe they have found Britain's oldest working cross-channel port, dating back to the Iron Age, at Poole Harbour in Dorset. Wooden support posts of oak, yew and birch found in two stone and rubble jetties have been radio-carbon dated to about 250BC. Professor Tim Darvill, head of Bournemouth University's archaeology group, said that the port would have been able to accommodate the biggest ocean-going boats of the day, which would not only have come from across the Channel, but may have also come from the Mediterranean. 'Imports would have included wine, spices and olives. And because of the good quality clay here, exports would have included pottery.' The jetties are believed to have been in use for about 300 years, but would have been under water soon after the Roman invasion.

Summary

One doesn't need to be a scholar to work out from all this evidence that much of the established community beliefs of the Palaeolithic, Mesolithic, Neolithic, Bronze Age and early Iron Age revolved around a respect for death, the ancestors, nature and the solstices. In *A Phenomenology of Landscape*, Christopher Tilley expounds his belief that the prehistoric landscape reflected the beliefs, myths, legends and stories of the period: for instance, when sunset at the Summer Solstice coincides with a chink in the hills on the skyline. At other times it may be more local or intimate, such as when an ancestral burial mound is, or is not, visible behind something as insignificant as a low hillock, or indeed another barrow. 'Either way, the play, the player and the landscape that once lived in all of their minds, are inseparable.'

What Francis Pryor also makes abundantly clear is that prolonged and elaborate funeral rites didn't suddenly appear 6,000 years after the Palaeolithic era with the arrival of the Neolithic people. This is when we have the introduction of farming and houses, and a more settled style of life; it is also when we find the first large communal tombs, barrows and other evidence for people coming together to mark or celebrate rites of passage. 'The social processes, and in particular the human need to mark a person's passing in this special way, have roots which go down very deep.'

What we know for certain about the beliefs – magical, mystical and religious – of the prehistoric peoples of these islands is that from a very early period, there was a strong sense of afterlife and/or ancestor worship, which suggests a shamanic approach in religious outlook. It is also highly suggestive from the colossal building projects carried out by people using only flint tools and reindeer picks, that the later religion was predominately patriarchal in structure, rather than matriarchal. The large monuments, treasure-stuffed burial mounds and artwork support the idea that Neolithic culture sustained an exceptionally highly developed astronomer-priesthood, and a taste for ceremonial. Does this suggest a two-tier system similar to that of ancient Egypt and Rome, with the State religion and the faith of the individual running in tandem?

By the middle of the Bronze Age, however, there had been a subtle shift from communal to individual burials, which points to the deceased being equipped for a journey into Otherworld – and the deceased followed their path alone. Nevertheless, human remains were often buried beneath the floor of the houses so that the dead would remain in close proximity to the family. Ancestor worship (usually considered tribal and primitive), remained an integral part of their daily lives, strengthening and encouraging the bonds of kinship and honour within the community. From what we know of ancestor worship in the modern world, we see it as a form of personal discipline and morality, since any error of judgement could result in shame being brought down on the ancestral spirits who remain as 'guardians' over family fortunes.

The prehistoric calendar was obviously governed by the solstices and equinoxes, since many of the ancient monuments were purposely aligned with the summer and winter solstices. These times probably marked the feast days and/or times for large community ceremonies to celebrate an important part of the annual cycle. In the time of the hunter-gatherers, the men supplied enough meat for the family/tribe, while the women provided the substantial daily fare as the gathering side of the partnership. Later, when the people began to rely more on domesticated crops, the women's vital role as gatherers was undermined as they were given the secondary task of labouring in the fields. Those remnants of the hunter-gatherer society, together with the tribal shaman, would probably have been pushed further back into the more inhospitable parts of the landscape, as large tracts of forest were cleared for the purposes of agriculture and encroaching domestication, thus creating the first 'them and us' divide in British society.

Symbols of rank were reflected in the variety of the grave goods and because of their rarity value, amber and jet would have been given a higher significance than as mere decorative objects. Baltic amber was found at Gough's Cave and it is interesting to speculate how this material found its way to Britain as far back as the Upper Palaeolithic and Mesolithic periods, although it is possible for it to have been washed from the Baltic seabed to the shores of Britain. Jet is known to have been mined since c1400BC; the finest in the world being found along the coast around Whitby, and in some shale deposits in other parts of Yorkshire. Less rare, ivory coming from the teeth and tusks of large wild animals has been used for personal adornment since the dawn of mankind – one piece of carved mammoth tusk found in France is more than 30,000 years old.

The image of a horse's head carved on a fragment of horse rib from Robin Hood's Cave, Creswell Crags, and dating from the Late Upper Palaeolithic era (1,200 years ago), reflects the ancient British respect for the horse, although it was more than likely to have been a food source long before its image was cut into the chalk hills at Uffington. Nevertheless, the horse must have generated some deep spiritual significance within early Britons for its influence to be carried so strongly in the genes of the 21st century Englishman, who demonstrates a marked aversion for eating horse-flesh – unlike his continental cousins who relish the meat.

'Not the least peculiar of the by-products of the human condition has been man's apparently irrepressible predisposition to create gods,' observes Michael Rice in *The Power of the Bull*. And nowhere else is this more appropriate than with the auroch (*Bos primigenius*), an 'immense beast standing two metres to the shoulder and weighing upwards of a tonne, of powerfully developed and co-ordinated flesh, muscle and bone'. This bull would have been a formidable opponent in the chase, and must have been the cause of the loss of life of more hunters than any other of their customary prey.

'The aurochs resisted the process of domestication, if indeed early sedentary man was ever foolhardy enough to attempt to tame a one-tonne bull with a metre-wide spread of horns ...' writes Rice, leading us to reflect that surely this image is more appropriate for a 'horned' god than the stag which is, after all, the ultimate prey animal. Whatever may have been the original reasons that made Upper Palaeolithic man and his successors invest the bull with so much symbolic importance – touching upon divinity – there can be little doubt that the animal came to occupy a unique place in the religious perceptions of *homo sapiens sapiens*, with the choice of the bull as the supreme sacrificial animal.

Similarly, perhaps we should also re-examine the 'water cult' – that most persistent of Pretanni beliefs, with offerings being made from the earliest times, through the Roman occupation and well into the Middle Ages. In fact, in Roman Britain the most famous water-cult centres at Aquae Sulis (Bath), whose names means 'the waters of the God Sul', and the monastery at Glastonbury, are believed to have been built over ancient water shrines. The custom of well-dressing survives up to the present day.

The Story So Far ...

As far as our 'home-grown' beliefs are concerned, all we can know with any certainty is that prior to the arrival of the Celts, the indigenous beliefs of the people were focussed on ancestor-worship and an afterlife, with the main points of the yearly cycle being observed at the solstices as indicated by the alignment of the numerous ancient monuments that litter the landscape. A more localised core of devotion was the attraction of 'watery places' such as springs and the water margins of lakes, fens and rivers: very similar, in fact, to ancient Shinto beliefs, which are still observed in Japan today. So far, we have the following points of similarity to ponder in relation to customs that *much later* became incorporated into traditional British Old Craft ...

- Of the few human remains excavated from the period, the style of burial and the accompanying grave goods point to a shamanic-type of tribal guidance. There was an emerging formal death-cult, closely aligned to what we now refer to as 'ancestor-worship' and which is still an integral part of modern Old Craft practice.
- Seasonal calculations were based on the solstices and equinoxes as sacred moments in the community calendar, as demonstrated by the alignment of the monuments. There was also a highly evolved astronomer-priesthood. The observance of the solstices and equinoxes remain the focal point of the modern Old Craft calendar, whereas in almost all other pagan 'wheel of the year' systems they have been relegated to 'lesser sabbats'.
- Personal adornment in the form of natural 'gems' such as amber, jet and ivory, left as grave goods, were probably used as amulets rather than as mere decoration. Amber and jet are still regarded as 'badges of rank' in some areas of traditional witchcraft.
- The earliest type of symbolism that has survived is the extensive use of circles, swirls, cup marks and spirals that occur on countless monuments and stone carvings.
- The depiction of animals in the form of art, cave paintings and carvings, particularly images of the horse, stag and bull, were probably adopted as some form of totem or clan representation. Different species of tree *may* also have served the same purpose. Many traditional covens have a

'clan totem' while individuals will have a personal 'power animal'.

- Bran is the only named pre-Celtic deity to have survived. His emblems are the alder tree and the raven.
- The sacredness of springs, fountains, wells and pools is still extant in Old Craft teaching.
- The ancient name for the indigenous people of Britain was the Pretanni, which has been translated as the 'painted people', or the 'tattooed ones', referring to the native penchant for decorative body-art. Some Old Craft groups still use a tattoo or brand as a badge of rank called 'the Mark'.

It would be a grave error of judgement, however, to claim that 'traditional' witchcraft can trace its origins back to pre-history, or that it is in some way the direct descendent of the old paganism – although this claim is often heard in pagan circles. What we *should* consider is the fact that witchcraft is an **ability within the individual** and in prehistoric times there would have been a growing recognition that some people had the remarkable skill of being able to heal, divine and conjour spirits. These trace elements of ancestral belief would also have entered the racial memory and somewhere, further down the line, another 'individual' with this *natural* ability would have connected with what they recognised as a 'magical truth' and incorporated it into their magical system.

There was no 'traditional' witchcraft in prehistoric times since what the people followed was the emerging religious beliefs of the time, with some form of shamanic mediation between the newly created gods and the tribe. Nevertheless, ancestral roots dig deep and there is obviously much that is buried in the Collective Unconscious that reflects the early beliefs of those distant days – after all, Old Craft has long been founded on 'instinct and intuition' and has never been static. In fact, the word 'witch' [*wicca* (mas) and *wicce* (fem)] dates from Old or Middle English, and what we should be looking at during this longest period of British history are shamanic practices that may originate as early as the Palaeolithic and certainly during the Neolithic period.

As we have seen, early **anthropological** evidence in caves and drawings on walls supports indications that shamanism started during the Palaeolithic era. **Archaeological** evidence exists for Mesolithic shamanism, with the oldest known female shaman's grave in the world being located in the Czech Republic. Nevertheless, with the current leaps and bounds in anthropological and archaeological research into our native heritage, we have no excuse for neglecting the **history of the time to which we feel instinctively drawn.** Those with witch-blood in their veins will pick up on those 'strange things lost and forgotten in obscure corners of the newspaper ...' and rediscover some other magical trace elements that link us to the ancient past.

Chapter Three

Lux Æterna for Five Masked Players (Invaders)

The essence of the lie is to be found in its deception, not its words.
Book of Grammayre

By the Later Iron Age (200BC-43AD), the migratory peoples from the European mainland were establishing themselves in Britain in increasingly large numbers. The newcomers integrated with the indigenous peoples, with a gradually increasing overlap of cultural ideas and identity. Where the concentration of newcomers was the stronger, the native culture would have been submerged, absorbed or obliterated.

For example, the alder, a tree highly suited to that primitive waterlogged landscape, was originally sacred to the indigenous god Bran; later included as one of the seven Celtic Chieftain Trees but displaced by the ash following the 'Battle of the Trees'. This suggests that it was sacred long before the Celts came to Pretannia. The alder is also described as 'the very battle-witch of all woods, the tree that is the hottest in the fight' (*The White Goddess*), suggesting that it may have been a military standard or clan totem belonging to the native people. We know that the Druids were associated with the oak tree ...were other native trees also symbolic of tribal or clan identity? What is beginning to emerge, is that later invading cultures apparently preserved many of the Pretannic customs within their own folklore ...

The Celts

Most of us were taught that the Celts had invaded Britain at various times during the Iron Age but modern archaeology is now at odds with this long-standing belief. Current excavations indicate that there was no full-scale invasion, bringing with it new styles of art, pottery, weaponry and jewellery; and that the newcomers lived in the same localities as those they were supposed to have ousted. In fact, in *The Atlantic Celts: Ancient People or Modern Invention?* Simon James argues that the Celts themselves probably never existed as a distinct cultural identity.

As to the question of when did the Celts arrive in Britain, Barry Cunliffe's response is now the most popular: 'The only way to re-phrase it and still retain the spirit of the enquiry is: 'At what stage and by what process did the language group commonly referred to as 'Celtic' reach, or emerge in, western Europe?''

And the answer?

The earliest reference we have of the Celts, or *Keltoi,* is by Herodotus, from the mid-fifth century, who mentioned them only briefly. According to David Miles, Research Fellow of the Institute of Archaeology, Oxford: 'Putting together the scraps of evidence from various Greek authors it seems likely that 'keltoi' was a name applied generally to the barbarian tribes of northern and western Europe ... in much the same way as later Europeans classified the indigenous people of mainland America as 'indians'. This is not the name these people originally used to describe themselves ... in similar fashion 'Celt' is a category identified by the ancient Greeks, and under their influence adopted by the Romans.'

In *The Tribes of Britain,* Miles goes on to explain that in 'more recent times the Celts have been romanticised into mystical and musical denizens of a never-never land', and as the scholar J R R Tolkien observed: 'Anything is possible in the fabulous Celtic twilight, which is not so much a twilight of the Gods as of the reason.' Other contemporary sources have attributed to the Celts a vast territorial influence that reshaped the face of Iron Age Europe and blotted out anything that had existed before. 'We are on more secure ground when using 'Celtic' to describe a family of *languages* ... that were spoken across much of western Europe,' concludes Miles. This example is still noticeable today by the differences between the Celtic languages of the Scottish and Irish (Gaelic) and Welsh, Cornish and Breton (Brythonic).

The earliest mention of the British Isles, however, occurs in later references to the *Massalliot Periplas*, written around 600BC, which describes a sea voyage from Marseilles. Great Britain is named 'Albion' and Ireland is 'Ierne' – both Celtic words. Another name comes from both old and modern Welsh, where the word for Britain is 'Prydain' – the ancient name for the indigenous people of Pretannia was the Pretanni, which as we have stated earlier, probably means the 'Painted People', or the 'Tattooed Ones', referring to the native penchant for decorative body-art that is still evident today in some Craft traditions.

So if there were no great invasions during the Iron Age, how did the Celts reach Britain? And what about the distinctive art-forms that appeared around this time?

According to Francis Pryor [*Britain AD*], the movement of both people and art did not involve a mass migration of people, and all the evidence for a vast pan-European culture simply isn't there. His answer is that they didn't come from outside, they were already here ... Certainly people were moving around, as they have always done and will continue to do but, he maintains, there is no evidence for large-scale, concerted folk movements in the fifth to third centuries AD.

If you examine a given tract of landscape, as I have done in the Peterborough area over the past 30 years, there is no sign whatsoever that the population changed some time in the mid-first millennium BC with the arrival of the Celts. It simply did not happen. Everything, from the location and arrangements of fields, settlements and religious sites to ceremonial rites, bespeaks continuity.

By the Late Iron Age and into the first years AD, Roman authors recorded that the Druidic religion flourished in Britain; the Romans saw this as a distinct threat and after their conquest made a determined effort to stamp it out, culminating in a battle and massacre on Anglesey in 59AD. Our knowledge of Celtic religious practice, however, remains 'in a state of the most rudimentary vagueness' and even the word 'Druid' has been open to much discussion. Current opinion, however, seems to agree with the ancient scholars, who related it to the Greek word for an oak-tree, *drus* (coupled with the Indo-European root *wid* – 'to know') and a tree-word would be appropriate for a religion with sacred groves in the deciduous mixed-oak forests of Europe.

The Celts had hundreds of names for gods and goddesses, each tribe having its own deities, which probably had different local names, although they were universal in type. As Stuart Piggott observes in *The Druids*, it would be rash to call all horned gods Cernunnos, or even perhaps all stag-antlered ones, since a count made some years ago showed that of 374 Celtic god-names then known from inscriptions, 305 occurred only once each, and only four or five of the remainder had totals of from 20 to 30 occurrences. 'To confuse matters more, when barbarian and classical deities are equated in dedicatory inscriptions, one Roman god may have the basic attributes of several Celtic divinities: an extreme example being the 69 Celtic god-names joined with that of Mars.' In addition, there is no way of knowing which were pure Celtic deities, or whether some had been integrated with even older god-forms of the Pritanni, to develop into the rich mythological cycle we know today.

The bulk of available information about the Celtic religion belongs to a much later phase in history, after Gaul and Britain had become part of the Roman Empire. The Druids, holding to a non-literary oral tradition, which was the time-honoured and socially approved method for the transmission of law, genealogy, story, song and myth, were 'specifically concerned with the preservation and continuance of this ancient convention, which avoided the use of writing'. Even later representations and inscriptions are cryptic, insomuch as suggesting some vague totemic association between various Celtic deities and animals – Cernunous the stag-antlered man; the boar, Baco; and Gaulish equine goddess Epona (who was adopted by the Roman cavalry).

The priesthood was made up of 'men of learning' (*druids*), bards (*bardoi*) and seers or diviners (*vates* or *manteis*), who appear to have been itinerant and inter-tribal, passing freely across the boundaries that separated one tribe from another. As repositories of the oral tradition, their presence was no doubt important at the periodic gatherings where old and new laws were proclaimed, especially since these public open-air meetings were often held at ancient tumulus-cemeteries or similar sacred sites.

The Fire Festivals, now an integral part of the modern traditions, were probably a Celtic innovation, although just how much of this folklore is genuine, is impossible to say. For example: the Furry Dance, which is still held on the nearest Saturday to the Feast of St Michael (8th May), may derive from the Celtic *feur*, meaning a holiday or fair. (It could, however, equally derive from the Middle English word *ferrie*, implying a Church festival.) The seasonal setting suggests that the dance may once have been a pagan spring festival, and the ceremony that precedes the Furry Dance is probably more significant than the dance itself. Known as the Hal-an-Tow, this mumming-play features the older children and is obviously a true relic of the ancient May games, designed to greet the summer with song and drama to induce crop fertility. Garlanded and carrying branches of sycamore, the participants sing an ancient song, part of the chorus of which runs:

Welcome is the Summer, the Summer and the May-O,
For Summer is a-come-O, and Winter is a-gone-O

The Celts recognised only two seasons – winter and summer.

Summer was seen to have arrived when the 'may' (the blossom of the hawthorn) was coming into bloom, which was when the cattle were turned out to pasture. Winter followed the gathering in of the harvest, when the cattle were brought back to the farmstead and surplus stock culled to provide meat for the long, cold winter months to come.

The Celts may, however, have given British mythology its stories about giants. When they arrived they saw the great stone circles and monuments left by earlier peoples and probably imagined them to be the work of some super-human race. Such tales grew with the passage of time and the legends survived long enough to be written down (and with much embellished) by Geoffrey of Monmouth (c1100-c1155), in his *History of the Kings of Britain*, but there is no archaeological evidence for associating Druidic ritual performances with Stonehenge, or any other stone circle of earlier date.

There is, however, a Gallo-Brythonic word *nemeton*, which is used for a shrine or sanctuary in a sense that implies a sacred grove or clearing in a wood, for the Celts had no concept of a temple in terms of man-made architecture. The woods and forests were their holy places. Even as late as the 8th century the Church was still denouncing those rites of prayer and magic which propitiated the secret powers of the forest depths and the forest soil. Many *nemeton* place-names existed in the Celtic world from Medionemeton in southern Scotland, to Vernemeton, between Lincoln and Leicester, while Aquae Arnemetiae, the modern Buxton, links the thermal spring and the sacred grove.

Nevertheless, bones from a remarkable find at Llyn Cerrig Bach (Anglesey) demonstrate that this ancient British 'water-cult' was still being observed, in the form of votive offerings, well into the Roman era. Radio-carbon dating of the bones shows that the lake was a long-term sacred spot, from at least 500BC until as late as 100AD. Francis Pryor (*Britain BC*) writes:

All the components of a heroic warrior culture are here at Llyn Cerrig Bach, from feasting to fighting, but there are other themes we have encountered earlier: water and the next world, travel and the final journey. The realm of the ancestors still exerts a powerful influence on the daily lives of ordinary people ... The careful destruction of the swords and other items suggests that they have been deliberately removed from circulation in this world, a rite that has its origins in the Neolithic, if not earlier.

Although Druids are believed to have existed throughout Celtic societies in Europe during the Iron Age, almost all surviving evidence of them is found in the writings of later Roman authors. Julius Caesar wrote one of the first and most detailed accounts, which explained that along with the rank of 'knight', the Druids were the highest-ranking order in Gallic society. His account also said that they 'engaged in things sacred' and functioned as law-givers, dispensing rewards and punishment in the case of murder, or disputes of land, or inheritance.

The Celts also displayed a strong belief in the afterlife as Caesar himself observed: 'Funerals, considering the standard of living, are splendid and costly; everything, even including animals which the departed is supposed to have cared for when alive, is consigned to the flames.' Pomponiu Mela in the first century AD makes the same point: 'They burn or bury with the dead the things they were accustomed to in life.' Posidonius recorded that the Celts held that 'the souls of men are immortal, and that after a definite number of years they live a second life when the soul passes to another body', while Strabo added that they believed that 'men's souls and the universe are indestructible, although at times fire and water may prevail'.

In addition to votive offerings, the Celts were favourably disposed to human sacrifice and this is what is supposed to have been behind the eventual brutal suppression and massacre of the

Druids by the Romans, who were themselves no strangers to wholesale slaughter – for amusement! Classical writers recorded that Druid ceremonies centred on human sacrifice (later made famous by the film image of *The Wicker Man*), also described by Caesar as *immani magnitudine simulacra*. Tacitus wrote: 'They deemed it a duty to cover their altars with the blood of captives and to consult their deities through human entrails.' By the early first century AD measures had been taken by a succession of Roman emperors to destroy the religion, but the name 'Druid' in the debased sense of a magician or prophet lingered on. Pliny's last work states that up to the 'present day Britain is still fascinated by magic, and performs rites with such ceremony that it almost seems as though it was she who imparted the cult to the Persians [then acknowledged as the masters of magic in the ancient world]'.

From the historian's point of view, the Celts of popular myth are an 18th century invention, but despite the brutal Roman suppression, Druidry was destined to make another comeback ...

NB: It is important to understand that human sacrifice was not confined to the Druids, or anyone else from that time. In her book *Dying for the Gods*, Professor Miranda Aldhouse Green shows that this practice was common throughout Iron Age and Roman Europe.

Romans

When the Roman armies swept through the empire they also carried a multitude of deities with them, like the contents of a gigantic shrimping net. The Roman army was made up of large numbers of foreign mercenaries, particularly those who were sent to the far-flung outposts of the empire. According to Readers Digest *Folklore, Myths and Legends of Britain*, a factor that aided the emergence of the different religious viewpoints was the number of Celts in the Roman army: by the end of the 2nd century AD about three-quarters of the Roman army in Britain was composed of Celts, though most of them came in from the Continent.

Agricola, who had the job of Romanising the ancient Britons between 77AD and 84AD, didn't pick on the chiefs: he educated their sons and, as Boris Johnson points out in *The Dream of Rome*, it became a mark of distinction to be seen wearing the toga – and gradually the war-like Britons embraced the creature comforts of Roman life. They also changed their beliefs about the dead and the way they dealt with the corpses of their loved ones. The Romans, however, didn't mind which gods they worshipped … the adherence to Taranis, Epona and Sucellus was just as proper as the belief in Mars, Apollo and Minerva … they stipulated only that observance should be made with proper Roman religious sensibility.

The Romans, always hedging their bets as far as foreign deities were concerned, accommodated the Celtic deities into their own pantheon and a subtle hybrid of north European and Mediterranean beliefs resulted from this blending of cultures and religious traditions. Even Julius Caesar wrote: 'About these gods they [the Celts] hold nearly the same views as other people do', and as a result there was sufficient common ground to 'permit fusion in a number of their respective deities'. In time, the Celtic war-god Cocidius became Mars-Cocidius, the healing-god Maponus became Apollo-Maponus, and so on.

There are also Latin inscriptions and written records that mention a water-deity, Arnmecta (or Arnemetia), the 'goddess beside the sacred grove', who was worshipped by the local people. Inscriptions to her have been found at Brough and at Buxton, where her shrine was located around the thermal spring. This connection was later developed by the Romans and, in Britain, was only second in importance to the great temple complex of Sulis-Minerva at Aquae Sulis (Bath). The name survived into medieval times when the springs became the focus of a holy-well cult and dedicated to a Christian saint, St Anne.

In Britain, the Romans also found the familiar concept of the

Matres or Matronae (Mothers) widely worshipped, often in a triple form and easily identified with their classical deities. According to Potter and Jones (*Roman Britain*), there are some 50 known dedications to the Mothers recorded in stone inscriptions and other objects, which constitute ample evidence of the importance of the cult among native Celts and others. They also make another interesting point:

> The Celtic horned god most often referred to by modern commentators was called Cernunnos. He has been equated with a horned deity often depicted sitting cross-legged and wearing a torc. It should perhaps be stressed that the name Cernunnos occurs only on *one single* incomplete inscription from Paris, and the god may have been known under many names ... Images of horned gods occur in Roman Britain, and we can infer that they symbolise the male side of the basic fertility cult. Many of the stone reliefs are too simple to tell us much about the identity of the god.

The Romans also drew a fine line between State religion and family observances, where it was still a recognised practice to make daily offerings to the ancestral spirits who took care of the domestic hearth. Some authorities regard the *lares* (household gods) as being originally rustic spirits who were transferred into the home when urban development expanded. It would have been this more personalised belief that the ordinary Romans brought with them to Britain, but few native Britons would have come into contact with these domestic gods, despite the similarity with their own ancestral worship.

The cosmopolitan Roman influence wasn't confined to the south of Britain as archaeological discoveries of a late Roman cemetery in Yorkshire have shown. A senior archaeologist at English Heritage, Dr Peter Wilson, has described the findings discovered close to present day Catterick, in *Cataractonium:*

Roman Catterick and its Hinterland. Although the excavations began in 1958 and carried on until 1998, the significance of many of the finds has only recently come to light.

One of these was the grave of a castrated priest who dressed in women's clothing, together with a matching jet necklace and bracelet, shale armlet and bronze expanding anklet. The remains were originally thought to be a woman when they were first discovered in the 1980s. Subsequent tests revealed that the skeleton was that of a young, slightly built man although the cause of death is not apparent. What is even more interesting is that the experts believe him to be a eunuch of the fertility cult of the goddess Cybele, who was imported from Anatolia in the 3rd century BC, and who subsequently became a Roman State deity, despite the rather unsavoury nature of her rites.

'In life he would have been regarded as a transvestite and was probably a *gallus*, one of the followers of the goddess Cybele, who castrated themselves in her honour,' explained Dr Wilson. 'He is one of the few Roman eunuchs ever discovered in Britain and highlights how even the northern-most reaches of the empire were relatively cosmopolitan 1,700 years ago.'

Some of the most convincing evidence for the survival of older beliefs can be dated back to the time of the Roman occupation. In the Peak District and at Hadrian's Wall, where soldiers were garrisoned, there are repeated finds that indicate a merging of traditions between the native British people, the Romans and their Celtic mercenaries. A number of curiously carved stones have been discovered in the valleys of the Peak District, which possibly represent the Celtic-Romano deities from that unsettled period of history. In fact, there is evidence to show that nearly every classical deity made an appearance in the British Isles in the form of sculpture or jewellery during this period, not to mention gods from far-flung Persia (Mithras) and Egypt (Isis).

This cultural overlay is aptly demonstrated by the largest

geophysical survey carried out in Britain, which has revealed an entire prehistoric Roman and Anglo-Saxon landscape where none was previously known to exist. 'Anglo-Saxon settlements, lost for a thousand years, together with evidence of Bronze Age, Iron Age and Roman ribbon-development up to 12 miles long have been found in the Vale of Pickering, North Yorkshire which, in effect, rewrites the archaeology of the settlement of Britain. The area is sand covered with a layer of loam, which has protected the prehistoric developments,' reported the Environment Editor of the *Daily Telegraph*.

On a more modest scale, the discovery of a 3rd century Roman village in Northamptonshire reveals a much more interesting time-capsule. According to a spokesman from Oxford Archaeology, the most important areas are the two shrines. One is a walled enclosure, and hundreds of items were found in this area, including brooches, pins and other offerings. A lot of the pieces had been ritually broken and deposited in the shrine, and arranged around a clearing in the centre. Along with fragments of pottery, bone and metalwork, the team found slabs of lead, which resemble 'curse tablets'. These have yet to be deciphered and may reveal the names of the gods being worshipped at the shrine that would have been used by both locals and travellers. A later shrine and temple, in the middle of a 'village green' have also been found. The dig has revealed something about how the dead were treated in Roman Britain: two main cemetery groups with a mixture of cremations and burials. Some heads had been removed and placed between the legs – a practice the Romans believed speeded up the passage into the afterlife. The village became deserted around the turn of the 4th-5th century as the Saxons arrived.

The Calendar

The Romans also introduced one of the most socially modernising concepts into the ancient British way of life. This innovation 'injected a new spirit into how people thought about time'. Before it had been thought of as a cycle of recurring natural events but now it became a practical tool by which people could organise their lives. Everything from growing crops to religious observances could be planned a long way ahead. 'The new Julian calendar introduced the concept of human beings ordering their own individual lives along a linear progression operating independent of the moon, the seasons and the gods,' observed David Ewing Duncan in *The Calendar*. Each day was dedicated to the observances for the various different gods (both State and domestic) and important landmarks in Roman history.

At the time of its inception (1st January 45BC), the Julian calendar was among the most accurate in the world, but it was still subject to 'tinkering by priests and politicians'. Periodically the calendar was rejigged to suit political whims and slippages of time, right up until the reforms of Pope Gregory XIII in 1582, and the introduction of the Gregorian calendar. Needless to say, not everyone under Roman domination suddenly abandoned the age-old ways of using the moon, stars and changes in the seasons. These changes to the way time was calculated would have only applied to the administrative and civic centres, and would not have affected the vast majority of rural people dwelling inside the borders of the empire.

On 4th October 1582, however, the introduction of the Gregorian calendar immediately stole ten days from people's lives and resulted in all the old festivals being moved forward by ten days – which goes a long way to explain why many of the modern 'revivalist' dates no longer align with the natural cycle of the year. In fact, only staunchly Catholic countries obeyed this latest Papal edict, and it took another 170 years before Britain finally adopted the new calendar, it being one of the last major European countries to do so.

The Abbots Bromley Horn Dance best demonstrates an

example of the way the newly introduced method of calculating time altered events in the folk-calendar. This has been described as 'the most primitive dance in Europe', and is still performed annually in the Staffordshire village on the Monday following the first Sunday after 4th September. In his *Natural History of Staffordshire* [1686], however, Robert Plot records that it was performed within living memory at Christmas, New Year and Twelfth Night ... suggesting that it was originally a Winter Solstice custom. It is not recorded why the celebration was moved, but the nature of the Horn Dance suggests an association with sympathetic hunting magic.

While the merchants and administrators in Roman commercial centres readily embraced the use of the calendar, it was the Church calendar that affected the lives of ordinary folk. Systematically, the clergy allocated the celebration of local traditions and festivals to 'ecclesiastical observances and commemorations of martyrs and saints'. The Church's liturgical year now began with the season of Advent and may have been an attempt to wean converts away from the pagan midwinter celebrations. Advent was first mentioned in Spain and Gaul and did not reach Rome until the 5th century, but it soon became a preparation for Christmas as a counterpart of the Lenten fast before Easter, though it was kept with less strictness.

By the 5th century the 'vast panoply' of Roman and Celtic gods had (in theory) been replaced by the official State religion of Christianity. Emperor Constantine, a last-minute convert, had decreed: 'By the unanimous judgement of all, it has been decided that the most holy festival of Easter should be everywhere celebrated on one and the same day'. Easter was now the principal event in the liturgical year, but this pagan festival of the Saxon goddess of spring, Eostre, remained (and remains) a movable feast, falling on the first Sunday following the first full moon after the Spring Equinox, and leading up to the time of the old Celtic Beltaine.

The Roman Lupercalia and the Celtic Imbolc were transformed into the Feast of the Purification of the Virgin Mary on
2nd February (commonly called Candlemas); while Roodmas
(the Mass of the Cross) on 30th April replaced the ancient
fertility festival of Beltaine, in an attempt to banish the bawdy
pagan influence from the revels. The Nativity of St John the
Baptist (24th June) replaced the Summer Solstice festival (21st
June), and the choice of August (15th in the south) and
September (8th in the north) for the principal Marian Festival
(the Assumption of the Blessed Virgin Mary), gave it a seasonal
significance inasmuch as its celebration coincided with the
gathering of the harvest, i.e. Lammas (Loafmas), or the Celtic
Lughnasad (1st August).

With the approach of the Autumn Equinox (21st September),
when the sun's weakening rays were becoming more apparent;
with the reciprocal effects in nature and men's thoughts turning
to death and gloom, the Feast of St Michael was introduced on
29th September to symbolise the autumnal struggle with the
forces of darkness and death [*Seasonal Feasts and Festivals*, E O
James]. The 31st October was set apart as All Saints and All Souls
for the commemoration of the saints, largely to Christianise the
pagan Samhain (Hallowe'en) and supplant the autumnal pagan
rites.

Christianity

In *Seven Ages of Britain*, Justin Pollard remarks that the only way
to get on in late Roman society was to be at least nominally
Christian: 'It was as important for your career then as it was to
hold a Communist Party card in 1930s Russia.' Once the Romans
left Britain, however, within little more than a generation, the
populace had returned to a pagan, rural society that only
differed slightly from the way it had been 400 years before. 'The
old religion, only ever lightly covered by a veneer of Roman and
then Christian ritual, re-emerged ... It was almost as though the

Roman invasion had never happened, except for their monumental ruins that littered the landscape.'

But all that was soon to change. When Pope Gregory sent Augustine to convert the heathen Anglo-Saxons in the 6th century, he told him:

> Do not pull down the fanes [temples]. Destroy the idols, purify the temples with holy water, set relics there and let them become temples of the true God. So the people will have no need to change their place of concourse, and where of old they were wont to sacrifice cattle to demons, thither let them continue to resort on the day of the saint to whom the Church is dedicated, and slay their beasts, no longer as a sacrifice but for a social meal in honour of Him whom they now worship.

As a result there is a medieval church built right inside a Neolithic circle at Knowlton in Dorset; Fimber church, in Yorkshire, stands on a Bronze Age barrow, which had also been used as an Anglo-Saxon burial place; and there is the ruin of a church tower on top of Glastonbury Tor. In order to preserve the continuity of local worship, the church grafted pagan symbols and legends onto the stories of the saints; in this way Christian blessings were given to the ancient pagan festivals. Many pagan altars and carvings were incorporated in the walls of churches, and even used as fonts. An altar dedicated to the Celtic god, Ocellus, can be found in the church porch at Caerwent, Monmouthshire; a Romano-British altar decorated with bulls stands within the church at Stone in Oxney, Kent; while the wall inside the church at Kirby, Underdale, in Yorkshire, boasts a relief of a Celtic war-god.

Although the old gods had been outwardly ousted from their temples, springs and sacred groves, they continued to thrive in the form of the music and dance of mumming. In remote pre-history, these magical dances were performed to pacify and honour the deities that the people believed controlled every aspect of their daily lives, with the dancers clad in animal skins or greenery. Such pagan practices were anathema to the early Church but just as the temples and feast-days had been absorbed into Christianity and the Church calendars, so the saints and biblical prophets were introduced into the drama.

Despite the efforts of the clergy, however, this was one area where they never succeeded in ousting the old pagan elements, which have survived (almost intact) to the present day. Mumming plays, whose origins are believed to be rooted in the oldest of pagan ceremonies, are still carried out by mummers all over England, despite the many varied regional variations; the most famous, as we have seen, being the Abbots Bromley Horn Dance. The mummers disguised themselves by blackening their faces or by wearing masks and garments made from ribbons, or strips of parchment, drawing on the ancient belief that if the dancers were recognised, the magical power would be invalid.

Summary

From a magico-religious point of view the Celts appear to have introduced the concept of the sacred grove as a meeting place and possibly the cauldron as a sacred vessel, although the *pre*-Celtic god, Bran, had a similar receptacle at his disposal. Although continuing the practice of using 'watery-places' for votive offerings, the focus suggests more of a shift towards specific Otherworld connections and sacrifice. Celtic deities for the first time were given 'names' that were identifiable and recorded by classical scholars, and which have, subsequently, been taken up by modern-day pagans. The Druids' acknowl-edged magical ability suggests that this practice was widespread, although the Romans were not interested in differ-entiating between the various 'barbarian' levels of society or ancestry, and conveniently lumped them all together.

The influx of scholars during the Roman era ensured that

much of what was 'strange and wonderful' in Iron Age Britain was recorded (albeit from the Roman perspective) if not understood, but there are no obvious dividing lines between the customs and culture of the indigenous people and the later arrivals. Magic and religion were still synonymous, but there is the general impression that the intermittent rites of the Neolithic astronomer-priesthood would not have found favour with the highly organised, community-based Druids, despite the magnificence of the former sacred sites. There is no record of what had happened to these learned men.

With the Roman occupation there also came such a multiplicity of gods and goddesses that all hope of being able to trace any tangible threads of indigenous Pretannic deities is very tenuous indeed. A large proportion of Roman soldiers serving in Britain were Celtic mercenaries, who had brought their own gods with them. So deities such as the horse-goddess Epona and even the Persian god Mithra found their way to these islands. When the legions left, however, to many of those with Romanian, French, Belgian or German ancestry, Britain was now their homeland and they melted into the countryside. No doubt many of their native customs were integrated into the new family life on a localised level, which man account for the diversity of traditions in different areas of the country.

The Story So Far …

The Celts' oral tradition meant that nothing was written down but passed 'from mouth to ear' in time-honoured fashion; it was the Romans who were the first to record their observations of the customs of these islands as we know from the writings of Tacitus and Strabo. In *Roman Britain* there is an interesting point concerning the co-existence and merging of the different beliefs of the time, which we would do well to ponder:

While it is clear that underlying Celtic and pre-Celtic beliefs and customs came to co-exist with imported classical paganism, it is not easy to unravel the different strands. This is partly because Celtic and Graeco-Roman paganism were based on the same fundamental concerns and preoccupations, those which form the basis of religion and superstition in all pre-industrial societies: namely the reverence and awe felt towards natural forces and the need to ensure the health and increase of humans, animals and plants. It was the rise of Christianity, with its emphasis on personal salvation, its vigorous proselytising and its total rejection of traditional beliefs, which led to serious tensions between varying religious systems. By comparison, Celtic and Roman paganism differed only in superficial detail.

Religion may be defined as a belief in some form of supernatural power, which influences or controls the lives of humans and the world of nature. And, like all pre-Christian cultures, the Celts and Romans would have had a profound belief in the magical aspects of their religion. In areas dominated by Celtic and Roman influence there may have been a noticeable number of Christian converts, but in remote places the Old Ways would have continued much the same as they had always done. For example:

- The comment made by Pliny that the British penchant for magic could outgun the Persians – then acknowledged as the masters of magic in the ancient world – reveals that magical practice was common and widespread among the *native British* population.
- The pre-Celtic belief that springs, watercourses and wells were mysterious and spirit-haunted places, has endured up to the present day (although more often than not the wells are now named for saints).
- The Celts may have utilised some of these native customs

and mingled them with their own beliefs, including the concept of the cauldron of knowledge/plenty.

- Native shamanic magical practices may have adopted many of the more ritualised customs introduced by the Romans, i.e. portents, divination and auguries; not to mention the *defixiones* (lead tablets used for cursing an enemy). Different forms of divination are still an integral part of Old Craft teaching.

- The native Pretanni tradition of 'body-painting' also persisted within Old Craft, being recorded in 1921 by Margaret Murray in *The Witch-Cult in Western Europe*, which suggested to her a tattoo as a badge of admission. The location on the body of the 'Mark' differed from location to location.

With the exception of the remaining Romano-British nobility, the majority of the people turned away from Romano-Christianity once the legions left. However, 350 years of Roman influence would have taken its toll on the expression of indigenous religious belief and magical practice, and the Christo-Roman love of organised ceremony probably had a long-lasting effect. With the departure of the legions, a large proportion of the urban populace reverted back to the Old Ways that were lying dormant just below the surface: water and the next world, a long-standing magical tradition, and 'the final journey'. The realm of the ancestors still exerted a powerful influence on the daily lives of ordinary people ... rites that had their origins in the Neolithic, if not earlier and preserved in the oral traditions of the 'incomers'.

Chapter Four

Night of Four Moons (The Dark Ages)

To them that ask thee, where has thou seen the Gods, or how knowest thou certainly that there be Gods, that thou art so devout in their worship? I answer first of all, that even to the very eye, they are in some manner visible and apparent. Secondly, neither have I ever seene mine own soule, and yet I respect and honour it. So then for the gods, by the dayly experience that I have of their power and providence towards my selfe and others, I know certainly that they are, and therefore worship them.
Marcus Aurelius, *Meditations*

The Dark Ages in Britain lasted from the official end of the Roman Empire to the mid-seventh century: 410AD-650AD – with the populace now being identified as 'emerging national identities'. As Francis Pryor remarks in *Britain AD*: 'The post-Roman period lurks on the misty, romantic fringes of that world. It's a period that we wish we could identify with, but sadly we cannot.' As a result, what the historians of the past didn't know, they sought to invent ... not from any desire to manipulate the truth, but to bestow legitimacy on a ruling house.

In 597AD, missionaries under St Augustine introduced the Roman Catholic version of Christianity to Britain and the pagan-Saxon period was followed by the Christian-Saxon period, which lasted right up to the Norman Conquest in 1066. The differences between the Augustine's Church of Rome and the singularly Celtic Church (that had been introduced separately by Irish and Breton missionaries, and which had developed independently since the Roman departure), were 'resolved' in order to bring the largely pagan populace back into the Church. This 'resolution' primarily came about by the massacre of 1,200 monks who had come from the monastery of Bangor-on-Dee to pray for victory for the princes of North Wales over Aethelfrith, the grandson of a heathen king much admired by Bede.

According to Bede, the monks of Bangor were heretics 'who learned through death the evil of their ways'. What Bede (and the Church of Rome) objected to was the fact that the Celtic clergy 'neglected' their pagan neighbours, insomuch that they made no effort to convert them to Christianity. In the *Historical Atlas of Britain* we find the following note: 'Nowhere do we hear of any attempt by the British clergy to convert the English, and even when the latter became Christian the British clergy maintained their distance: we hear of them refusing to worship besides Angles ... It is, therefore, no surprise that those who converted the English came from abroad.'

The Romans had introduced writing into Britain, but it was the contemporary chroniclers like Gildas (6th century – *Ruin and Conquest of Britain*); the Venerable Bede (c.731 – *Historia Ecclesiastica Gentis Anglorum*) and the *Anglo-Saxon Chronicles* (c.890) that provided the source material for later historians. It was, however, the highly influential author and creator of the dominant Arthurian legends, Geoffrey of Monmouth (c.1136), who told the story of Britain in his *History of the Kings of Britain* and muddied the waters right up until the present day.

According to Arthurian scholars in their introductions to the work, Geoffrey had a 'clear-cut political reason' for writing his *History*, and that was to give 'a precedent for the dominions and ambitions of the Norman kings and his wish to ingratiate himself with his various dedicatees'. At the beginning of the *History*, Geoffrey states quite categorically that Walter the Archdeacon presented him with 'a certain very ancient book written in the British language', which he translated into Latin. Unfortunately, there remains no trace or evidence of this book, neither is there any mention of a character called Arthur in any ancient account of Britain written between 400AD-820AD – and Arthur is supposed to have lived in the 5th century.

There are 6th and 7th century accounts of battles and other events from the 5th century, which modern authors have linked to Arthur ... but no one wrote about him by name until some four centuries later. The earliest account to link Arthur with actual events was written by a monk of the Celtic Church, Gildas. The first account of a person named Arthur can be found in the *Historia Brittonum*, which was written around 829-30 for the benefit of the north-Welsh king, Merfyn, in order to provide the Welsh with a 'heroic Celtic leader' to counter the 'Englishness' of Bede's history.

There is also the *Mabinogion*, a collection of tales drawn from Celtic mythology, with some details possibly harking back to older, Iron Age traditions. The *Mabinogion* is the product of a highly developed medieval Welsh narrative tradition, both oral and written [see *Wikipedia*] and in the mid 19th century, Lady Charlotte Guest was the first to publish English translations of the collection. The debate over the dates for the tales continues unabated, because if they can be shown to have been written *before* Geoffrey of Monmouth's *Historia Regum Britanniae* and the romances of Chrétien de Troyes, then it would provide important evidence for an earlier development of Arthurian legend. The tales appear in the *White Book of Rhydderch* (*Llyfr Gwyn Rhydderch* c1350), and the *Red Book of Hergest* (*Llyfr Coch Hergest* c1382-1410), though fragments have been preserved from earlier 13th century manuscripts. Scholars generally agree that the tales are older than the existing manuscripts, but disagree over just *how much* older.

In recent times, however, most of us have gleaned our impressions of this dark period of British history from that glorious epic fantasy: J R R Tolkien's *The Lord of the Rings*. Although this is a fictional tale of sorcery and spirit worlds, we should always bear in mind that Tolkien *was* a scholar (Professor of Anglo-Saxon at Oxford), and was the first to admit that the background for the saga of Middle-earth was not his own invention, but an old Anglo-Saxon term for the magical world inhabited by the people of the first millennium (0-100AD). And it is this culture, made up of the many colourful early European tribes now identified under the umbrella titles of Celts, Anglo-Saxons and Norse, on which he based *The Lord of the Rings.*

The Lord of the Rings trilogy has been referred to as 'the bible of alternative society', an observation that has brought derision from some quarters, who hasten to remind us that Tolkien's writings are not true! In fact, there are equally as many magical and moral truths in Tolkien's saga as in the Christian Bible, although the author simplified the numerous conflicting belief systems that abounded at the time. A considerable amount of contemporary pagan imagery is based on the Arthurian and Tolkienesque romances, and it would be easy to fall into the trap of wishful-thinking in wanting these fictitious tales to be Truth. So, just how real was the magical world of Merlin and Gandalf ...

Anglo-Saxons and Norsemen

As we have seen, the withdrawal of the Roman legions was quickly followed by the arrival of the Anglo-Saxons. Unlike the lowland regions to the south, these invaders had little impact on the upland people and any remaining native traditions probably passed down through the generations virtually unaltered, until the Industrial Revolution started the migration into towns. There are few traces of the great Teutonic gods left in Britain, but the gods of the later invaders made nothing like the same impact as the rich array of established Romano-Celtic deities. In any case, their reign was but a brief one: a century and a half later, 'the gods of Roman, Briton and Teuton alike yielded to the triumphant advance of Christianity' (*Britain AD*).

The earliest private chapel from the Dark Ages has been unearthed in the foundations of a Roman stately home. The 5th century font and baptistery were built onto the ornate mosaic floor of an unusually grand double villa in Wiltshire, not long after the Romans left Britain. Although there are older chapels, archaeologists say it is the earliest example of a landowner converting rooms inside his home for baptisms. A spokesman from Bristol University believes the villa was owned by a local Romanised British family, 'People who were already powerful before the Roman conquest, and who made the right decision at the time of the invasion ... by the end of the 4th century most of the wealthy and influential families would have embraced the new religion in Britain.'

Historians are only just beginning to unravel these so-called Dark Ages and to separate the differing strands between Anglo-Saxon and Norse culture that have previously been lumped together under a single banner. To the casual reader there is little difference because the similarities between them are so great and the differences so few, but as Pete Jennings, author of *Heathen Paths: Viking and Anglo Saxon Pagan Beliefs* wrote: 'I deplore the way in which it is presumed by many that Anglo-Saxon paganism was the same as Scandinavian, but with some slight changes (Odin to Woden, Thor to Thunor, Tyr to Tiw, etc.).' Writing from the standpoint of someone with an interest in both camps, he points out that the similarities weren't consistent from one village to another, let alone across several different countries.

But the influence of one Anglo-Saxon deity is still strongly felt today. Eostre, goddess of spring, from whose name the word Easter was derived, and the most sacred festival of the Christian calendar. According to George Ewart Evans in *The Leaping Hare*, the month of April was called Eostre-month, the dawn-month, and the pre-Christian festival included symbolic rites of death and resurrection. 'Few details are known, but there is no reason to think that it differed basically from other spring festivals ... The natural sequence of winter and summer, darkness and light was compressed in most spring festivals into a few hours or days.'

Eostre's companion animal and attendant spirit was the hare. Little else is known about her writes Ewart Evans, 'It has been suggested that her lights, as goddess of the dawn, were carried by hares. And she certainly represented spring fecundity, and love and carnal pleasure that leads to fecundity.' In fact, no animal in British folk and country-lore has gathered more mystery about itself than the wild hare, particularly in connection with witches and their familiars.

One such image is the circular motif of three hares that appears in sacred sites from the Middle and Far East, to the churches of southwest England (where it is referred to as the 'Tinners' Rabbits'), as an architectural icon and a religious symbol. The symbol features three hares chasing each other in a circle; two hares share each of the ears, so that only three ears are actually visible. Those who preserve the rural traditions have a healthy respect for the hare, with many who will hunt the animal but refuse to eat its flesh, even though they will eat rabbit. Perhaps the hare, like the horse and bull, is another sacred animal of the native Collective Unconscious?

There has been a long-held theory that claims the Anglo-Saxons were the root-source of most English folk-customs and beliefs – they may not have been the originators, but they were the first *recorders* of British cultural history. Veneration of wells and springs, curious seasonal customs and old ways of acknowledging nature continued in the outlying regions and uplands for hundreds of years – even into the latter part of the 20th century – as the high and often inaccessible uplands helped to preserve traditions, which had died out elsewhere in the land.

Nevertheless, Anglo-Saxon heroic poetry, such as *Beowulf, Sir Gawain and the Green Knight* and the *Battle of Maldon*, does deal with the traditions of an older world, and expresses another temperament and way of living. It 'breathes the influence of the wind and the storm-wrack', and according to *A Primer of English*

Literature, 'It is the poetry of a stern and passionate people,' concerned with the primal things of life, moody, melancholy, and fierce. The author claims there is an Homeric greatness about the poem *Beowulf,* which was originally pagan in tone, 'with the stern and dignified paganism of the old sagas,' but although attempts were made to Christianise it in the 8th century – much to the detriment of the original – it still weaves a vivid tapestry of Anglo-Saxon life. As does *Codex Exoniensis,* or *The Exeter Riddle Book* – the word 'riddle' deriving from the Old English *rædan,* to advise, to counsel, to guide or explain; and offering a poetic glimpse into the 'pagan Germanic world, survivals of the time before the Angles, Saxons, Frisians and Jutes first came to England ...'

The Christian monk and historian, the Venerable Bede, also preserved a considerable amount of data concerning Anglo-Saxon culture, writing about Sighere, King of the East Saxons, rebuilding ruined temples to restore 'heathen' worship after a serious outbreak of plague. The most significant pagan find of Anglo-Saxon period, however, is the 90ft longship found on a hill at Debden, Suffolk, in 1939, which contained 263 items of funerary regalia (including a splendid helmet, great shield and sword with its intricate gold sword-belt inlaid with garnets), believed to belong to the last pagan king of England, Raedwald, who died c625. The lack of any human remains is attributed to the highly acidic soil of the mound, which has broken down bone, as well as flesh, over the centuries.

This was the warrior-king of the East Angles and the first king of all the English peoples, whose temple (allegedly where Rendlesham church now stands in Suffolk) survived well into the era of Christian conversion. Royal burials went on in increasingly splendid style at Sutton Hoo for about 50 years until, just after Raedwald's death in about 625, the Anglo-Saxons were converted to Christianity and burial customs changed again. The royal mounds contained two ship burials (one of which was plundered by grave robbers in the 16th and 19th centuries), some cremations and the burials of a 25-year-old warrior and his horse, but no one knows why the method of burial varied so much. In Christian times the place was used for the execution of offenders, who were buried in 'grotesque attitudes'.

In *The Real Middle-Earth*, Professor Brian Bates admits that until recently, historians still tended to regard these people as 'primitive, violent and obscure barbarians ... but research in a wide range of disciplines is revolutionising our view of the past ...' These primary sources are necessarily varied and patchy for several reasons. One is that the Anglo-Saxon and Norse, in particular, wrote down little of their beliefs and traditions, since theirs were still mainly oral cultures. They told stories, some of which, fortunately, were written down at the end of the millennium, including the great Anglo-Saxon poem *Beowulf*. They memorised healing remedies, a small core of which were recorded by Christian monks and are available to us now, a thousand years later, in Anglo-Saxon documents such as the magical healing manuscript called *Lacnunga*, kept in the British Library. They used runes as symbolic writing for the magical purposes of divination and spellcasting. Other material comes from leech books and verse charms (*Nine Herbs Charms*), laws, the *Anglo-Saxon Chronicle*, letters and the Anglo-Saxon rune poem.

According to the entry for English witchcraft in *The Encyclopaedia of Witchcraft and Demonology*, by Rossell Hope Robbins, the concept of witchcraft in Anglo-Saxon times was damage done to crops or cattle caused by spells or poisons, and damage done to people ranging from causing sickness, sterility or death. In the early regulations, witchcraft involved 'a specific malicious act which could be seen and proved' – it was what witches *did* that counted, not what people thought they did. The first recorded legislation against witches occurred in the *Liber Poenitentialis* of Theodore, Archbishop of Canterbury (668-90), where a typical penance for divination was a prescribed period of fasting. Similarly, the *Confessional* of Egbert, Archbishop of York (735-66), demanded that a woman 'slaying by incantation' should fast for seven years. Witchcraft was seen as a crime against man rather than any crime against God, and the standards of evidence, the rules of the trial, and the penalties were the same as for any other anti-social act.

The missionaries left some remarkable accounts of these pre-Christian spiritual practices in the form of 'negative thought' from which we can read a positive print-out of early magical and spiritual traditions. One directive from an early Archbishop of York, for example, forbade the 'veneration of springs and magic involving dead bodies and omens and charms ... and the veneration of trees and stones'. The Council of Clovesho (c747) condemned those who practised divination, auguries, incantations, etc., while the *Dialogue* of Archbishop Egbert took exception to those who worshipped idols (naturally seen as trafficking with the Devil), auspices, astrology and enchantment.

The Laws of King Alfred of c880 deemed that women harbouring 'enchanters, wizards and witches' should not be allowed to live, echoing that old questionable chestnut of biblical translation: 'Thou shalt not allow a witch/poisoner to live ...' A similar fate awaited anyone discovered sacrificing to idols (i.e. the old gods).

King Athelston (925-39) made death the penalty for murder by witchcraft; King Edgar (c970) forbade well worship (a practice to be revived by the church in later times), divination and tree worship. While in edicts issued years apart, Wulfstan, Aelric and Cnut (c995) also imposed bans on 'animal guising', saluting the moon, making offerings at waterfalls, and oaths to heathen gods, which shows that the Old Ways were still persisting despite the growth of Christianity.

King Æthelred's laws passed between 1009-16 decreed that his people should renounce all pagan customs and 'exiling witches along with whores' – showing that it was still necessary to uphold the legislation passed by Archbishop Theodore some four centuries earlier, which banned pagan practices of sacrificing to 'devils' and divining the future. History shows, however, that it is impossible to legislate a belief out of existence and as pagan author Pete Jennings has pointed out, **it is highly unlikely that laws would be repeatedly passed against something that no longer existed!**

The Danelaw

The Romans came and went; and by now Leicester, Lincoln, Derby, Stamford and Nottingham made up the Five Boroughs, which were run by Danish soldiers during the 9th and 10th centuries. For 300 years, rule in the Boroughs was by Danelaw, which introduced for the first time in England the concept of guilt by majority verdict of a jury.

Although popular belief still harbours mental images of Vikings raping and pillaging, many of these Scandinavian people settled around the British Isles. The origins of the Danelaw arose from the Viking expansion of the 9th century, although the term was not used to describe the geographic area until the 11th century. With the increase in population and productivity in Scandinavia, Viking warriors, having sought treasure and glory in the nearby British Isles, 'proceeded to plough and support themselves', in the words of the *Anglo-Saxon Chronicle* for the year 876.

Danelaw is also used to describe the set of legal terms and definitions created in the treaties between King Alfred and the Danish warlord, Guthrum, written following Guthrum's defeat at the Battle of Ethandun in 878. In 886, the Treaty of Alfred and Guthrum was formalised, defining the boundaries of their respective kingdoms, with provisions for peaceful relations between the English and the Vikings. Ironically, the prosperity of the Danelaw subsequently led to its becoming a target for later Viking raiders and, together with the conflict with Wessex and

Mercia, its ultimate decline. The waning of its military power together with the Viking onslaughts led to its submission to Edward the Elder in return for protection, and the Norsemen gradually became Anglo-Scandinavians.

The formal treaties between the English and these Northern migrants meant that the Norse gods also integrated themselves with the growing British pantheon. The best source for Norse belief is given in the *Eddas* – the title given to two Icelandic books that provide the bulk of information available about Norse mythology. The *Elder* or *Poetic Edda* and the *Younger* or *Prose Edda*, were probably composed in Iceland in the early 13th century, and contain the myths and legends associated with the Norse gods and heroes.

Summary

There was now such a diversity of people in Britain that it must be looked upon as a truly multi-cultural society, with diverse and inseparable beliefs and folklore to match. During the early part of the millennium many of them would probably have retained their own tribal traditions, interwoven with the rites of the new religion – Christianity. Nevertheless, the old customs prevailed, maintaining strong links to superstition and the supernatural as we shall see:

Supernatural power means literally power above and beyond the forces of nature ... A belief in supernatural power is the basis of religion. It sets religion apart from the everyday world. Religion involves the creation of the sacred. When something is made sacred or sanctified, it is set apart, given a special meaning and treated with reverence, awe, respect and sometimes fear ... Religion includes a set of beliefs and practices which the faithful are required to hold and follow ... The influence of religion on social life can also be seen from religious festivals and ceremonies. Such events can unify people in society. In a religious ritual a social group comes together to express its faith in common values and beliefs ... The atmosphere is highly charged, emotions are touched and the ceremony is raised above the level of a normal social event ... By participating in a religious ritual people feel a part of something larger than themselves and become aware of the moral bonds which unite them.

[*Sociology*]

Once the pagan agricultural festivals and celebrations had been absorbed into the Church calendar, the local witch or wise-woman might even have been seen as a church-going, card-carrying member of the parish. This idea is borne out by the fact that, even today, some branches of traditional witchcraft persist in using the old Church calendar names for the major festivals that remained very much part of the agricultural year despite the repackaging. The supernatural powers of the Old Ways could still be followed under the protective powers of the Church.

The Story So Far ...

By this period, we can see that the magical and spiritual traditions involved healing remedies, the use of runes for the purpose of divination and spell-casting, omens and charms, the even then ancient custom of the veneration of springs, trees and stones, and 'magic involving dead bodies' (which we would probably interpret as ancestor/spirit worship/necromancy in its widest possible sense), was all classed as pagan practice and now roundly condemned by the Church.

- Many of the seasonal folk-customs integrated into the Church calendar were those that were so deeply embedded in the native psyche that they were eventually modified for Christian use; while the Church names for the festivals continued to be used in traditional witchcraft up to the present day.

- The introduction of ritual in religious observance within the Church probably encouraged local witches and cunning-folk to include a bit more psycho-drama into their own practice for the benefit of their clients, as well as the use of saints' names in a spell – another custom that has persisted down to the present day in traditional witchcraft.
- The existence of *identifiable* witchcraft has been recorded from Anglo-Saxon times. The introduction of strong laws governing its practise means that witches were not uncommon in the community, since no ruling body will legislate against something that is only an extremely rare occurrence. Nevertheless, it appears that we are looking at solitary 'wise women' rather than any formal gathering or grouping (i.e. coven) of witches at this point in time.
- The hare being recognised as a sacred animal within traditional witchcraft certainly dates from this time, although it *may* also have originated in a much earlier period. In modern Old Craft it is still forbidden to kill or eat the flesh of a hare.

Whether the 'witches' of the time had inherited any of the pre-Christian shamanic peoples' legacy, it is impossible to say, but the fact remains that witches didn't suddenly manifest as fully-fledged members of society with the arrival of the law-passing Anglo-Saxons ... and what had happened to the descendants of the pre-Celtic shaman, and of the astronomer-priesthood, whose ancestors had built Stonehenge and Avebury? If truth be told, they had probably always been there, concealed in the shadows, but with the growing population requiring healing and fortune-telling, their public presence possibly became more noticeable.

Those natural abilities that set one person apart from his or her neighbours also manifested in what were known as 'cunning-folk' – practitioners of folk magic from the medieval period through to the early 20th century. Primarily using spells and charms as a part of their profession, they were most commonly employed to use their magic in order to combat malevolent witchcraft, to locate criminals, missing persons or stolen property, fortune-telling, healing, treasure hunting and to cause people to fall in love. They were known by a variety of names in different regions of the country, including wise men and wise women, pellars, wizards, *dyn hysbys*, and sometimes white witches.

They also practised what is known as 'low magic' with a dash of 'high magic', which they learned through the study of *grimoires*. Ronald Hutton (*The Triumph of the Moon: A History of Modern Pagan Witchcraft*) describes them as belonging 'to the world of popular belief and custom', and defines their magic as being 'concerned not with the mysteries of the universe and the empowerment of the magus, so much as with practical remedies for specific problems'.

Chapter Five

Ancient Voices of Children
(Faere Folk and Folklore)

Myths in general are archetypal tales which once formed the
religious and historic consciousness of people ...
Patrick Crampton, *Stonehenge of the Kings*

The greatest contradiction relating to the Faere Folk is between
the modern view of them as miniature, iridescent creatures,
butterfly-winged and innocent as portrayed by Cicely Mary
Barker's *Flower Fairies*; and the traditional view that even the
kindest of them are dangerous. Some believe them to be spirits of
the dead, while to others they are memories of a long-lost people
who once inhabited these islands, which goes a long way to
explain why they are not particularly sympathetic towards
humans – especially those descending from the invading
peoples.

Belief has it that they were a small, dark-skinned people who
lived in the wild, uncharted places. In fact, there are many
differing theories about the origins of the Faere Folk, the most
common being the one mentioned by archaeologist Margaret
Murray in *The Witch-Cult in Western Europe:* that faeries were the
descendants of the early people of Northern Europe.

This connexion of witches and fairies opens up a very wide
field ... It is now a commonplace of anthropology that the
tales of fairies and elves preserve the tradition of a dwarf race
which once inhabited Northern and Western Europe.
Successive invasions drove them to the less fertile parts of
each country which they inhabited, some betook themselves
to the inhospitable north or the equally inhospitable

mountains; some however, remained in the open heaths and moors, living as mound-dwellers, venturing out chiefly at night and coming in contact with the ruling races only on rare occasions. As the conqueror always regarded the religion of the conquered as superior to his own in the arts of evil magic, the dwarf race obtained the reputation of wizards and magicians ... The identification of the witches with that fairy race would give a clear insight into much of the civilisation of the early European peoples, especially as regards their religious ideas.

The word 'fairy' derives from Middle English *faierie* (also *fayerye, feirie, fairie*), a direct borrowing from Old French *faerie*, meaning the land, realm, or characteristic activity (i.e. enchantment) of the legendary people of folklore and romance. The Modern English *fay*, meaning 'a fairy', is rarely used, although it is well known as part of the name of the legendary sorceress Morgan le Fay of Arthurian legend, and as the name of a character in the novels of Dion Fortune.

Gerald Gardner, writing in *Witchcraft Today*, describes the 'Little People' as being good friends and dangerous enemies, very strong, experts in magic and able to disappear at will, who were persecuted or banished by the Church. 'Witches consorted with them and they often intermarried, and became the fairy-kin of later legends.' In the Scottish witch-trials it was deemed that witches and faeries were one and the same; and that in England they were mostly pre-Celtic aborigines, among them many Romano-Britons who had stayed after the Saxon invasion.

The Faere Folk are generally described as human in appearance and having immense magical power, and much of the folklore about them revolves around protection from their malice, by such means as cold iron, or charms of rowan and herbs, or avoiding offense by shunning locations known to be theirs. In his manuscript, *The Secret Commonwealth of Elves, Fauns and Fairies,* Reverend Robert Kirk, minister of the Parish of Aberfoyle, Stirling, Scotland, wrote in 1691:

> These Siths or Fairies they call *Sleagh Maith* or the Good People ... are said to be of middle nature between Man and Angel, as were Daemons thought to be of old; of intelligent fluidous Spirits, and light changeable bodies (lyke those called Astral) somewhat of the nature of a condensed cloud, and best seen in twilight. These bodies be so pliable through the subtlety of Spirits that agitate them, that they can make them appear or disappear at pleasure.

Alan Richardson, writing the Prologue for the 2005 facsimile edition of *The Commonwealth,* observes that to 'the people of that time the faeries were not the tedious, pretty little thumb-sized creatures that they were reduced to by the Victorian imagination, but other-dimensional beings of real power, with their own laws, who co-existed (not always happily) with our own world, and who were linked with the ancient deities of forgotten faiths'.

To R J Stewart, faeries were real beings in their own right with substantial supernatural powers, and 'the *genius loci* of the ancient world'. He believed that the spirits of the dead and the ancestors also inhabited the world of the Faere Folk, although they were not of the faerie race; also that human spiritual or psychic healers worked through methods laid down by faerie tradition, 'often using corrupted prayers and incantations to accompany their healing ceremonies'.

Origin of the Faere Folk

A common theme found among the Celtic people also describes a race of diminutive people who had been driven into hiding by the invaders. They came to be seen as another race, or possibly spirits, and were believed to live in an Otherworld that was variously described as existing underground, in hidden hills (many of which were ancient burial mounds), in caverns by, or under, lakes or across the Western Sea.

In Scottish folklore, faeries are divided into the *Seelie Court*, the more beneficently inclined (but still dangerous) faeries; and the *Unseelie Court*, the malicious faeries. While the faeries from the *Seelie Court* enjoyed playing pranks on humans they were usually harmless pranks, compared to the *Unseelie Court* that enjoyed bringing harm to humans as entertainment.

Another popular belief was that they were the dead, or some subclass of the dead, since the Irish banshee (Irish Gaelic *bean sí* or Scottish Gaelic *bean shìth*, which both mean 'fairy woman') is sometimes described as a ghost. Many of the Irish tales of the Tuatha Dé Danann refer to these beings as faeries, though in more ancient times they were regarded as deities. The Tuatha Dé Danann were spoken of as having 'come from Islands in the north of the world', or in other sources, from the sky. After being defeated in a series of battles with other Otherworldly beings, and then by the ancestors of the current Irish people, they were said to have withdrawn to the *sídhe* (fairy mounds), where they lived on in popular imagination as 'faeries'.

The *Tylwyth Teg* (Welsh: 'the Fair Folk') is the common term in Wales for faeries. Right up until the early 19th century it was commonly believed that the Tylwyth Teg, described as ethereal, beautiful and fair-haired, still dwelt in a number of places in Wales as genii loci, such as the lake of Llyn y Fan Fach, and faerie paths upon which it was dangerous for a mortal to walk. They are usually portrayed as benevolent but capable of mischief; neither entirely good nor completely evil. In the marketplace at Bala, although no one could see the Tylwyth Teg, when the noise of the market rose to a roar, and the prices began to go up, everyone knew they were there. The writings of Arthur Machen often describe encounters with the more inhospitable nature of these Welsh Faere Folk, and serve as a warning not to interfere with them.

In alchemy in particular, they were regarded as elementals, such as gnomes and sylphs, as described by Paracelsus. This is uncommon in folklore, but accounts describing the faeries as 'spirits of the air' are not uncommon as Shakespeare described in *The Tempest*.

Faeries appeared frequently in medieval romances as one of the kinds of beings that a knight errant might encounter, but dwindled in number as the medieval era progressed; the figures became wizards and enchantresses. Morgan le Fay, whose connection to the realm of Faerie is implied in her name, in *Le Morte d'Arthur* is a woman whose magic powers stem from 'learning'. While somewhat diminished with time, faeries never completely vanished from the tradition. *Sir Gawain and the Green Knight* is a late translation, but the Green Knight himself is an otherworldly being. Edmund Spenser featured faeries in *The Faerie Queene*. The 15th century poet and monk John Lydgate wrote that King Arthur was crowned in 'the land of the fairy', and taken in his death by four faerie queens to Avalon, where he lies under a 'fairy hill', until he is needed again. Shakespeare's *A Midsummer Night's Dream* revolves around a cast of faerie characters.

In the Middle Ages, faeries feature in the legends about King Arthur, in the Border ballads and in medieval romance. Traditionally they were as tall as humans, but they could also be very tiny; like their human counterparts, they spent their time hunting, hawking and feasting. Stories of the period also told of the 'Faerie Rade', when they rode in procession on white horses, hung with silver bells. The story of Scotland's last *Fairy Rade* was told by the Scottish writer, Hugh Miller, more than 100 years ago. A herd-boy and his sister saw a procession of glittering strangers riding through a hamlet near Glen Eathie. As the last rider passed by, the boy asked who they were, and where they were going. 'Not of the race of Adam,' said the rider, turning for a moment in the saddle. 'The People of Peace shall never more be seen in Scotland.' This legend also has its echoes in *The Lord of the Rings*, where the elves are leaving Middle-Earth by ships from the Grey Haven, 'out into the High Sea and passed on into the West'.

But apparently not all of the Faere Folk left these islands. For hundreds of years, witches and faeries have been synonymous with each other, sharing the same magical attributes because faeries were believed to have interbred with humans to strengthen their stock. And from this interbreeding came the race of witches, which evolved into traditional British Old Craft in all its varied manifestations in various different strains across the British Isles. In Wales, the 'Fair People' played such a dominant part in Welsh folklore that they appeared as a parallel population of the country, and all folklorists agree on how completely people believed in their existence right up until the rise of popular education. In *Myths & Legends of Wales*, Tony Roberts also tells us that they were almost human, with faerie-women marrying humans and having children.

The tradition that iron gives protection against faeries may also have sprung from some dim memory of the Celtic invasion. The victorious Celts were armed with iron: the race they dispossessed had weapons of stone or bronze. Recent finds had revealed, however, that the native people were themselves accomplished metalworkers and many ancient finds have shown that while the people did not mine iron, they were familiar with meteoric iron – elf-bolts!

Protective measures that acted as a barrier against malignant faerie forces getting into the house included the placing of objects in the foundations or wall cavities, which acted as charms against intrusion. Although the practice dates back to the Middle Ages, superstitious homeowners were still concealing charms to ward off evil spirits as recently as the late 20th century. The location is usually under the floorboards or within the walls, and invariably close to doorways, windows or fireplaces because these were seen as the most vulnerable parts of the house where evil could enter.

The most common objects retrieved are old shoes, and 'witch bottles' – glass or stone bottles containing ingredients for some kind of protective charm – or animal remains including dried cats, horse skulls and skeletons of birds. Owners of houses and farms continued to rely upon traditional charms to protect their property and livestock from witches and faeries, and discreetly acknowledged the old turning of the seasons at May Day and All Hallow's Eve, which marked the beginning of summer and the start of winter.

Many explanations have been given to account for these persistent beliefs in the existence of the Faere Folk. Some sources (like Margaret Murray) suggest that they exist in their own right; while Victorian folklorists have suggested the Faere Folk were representative of the old pagan gods, symbolically reduced in stature and importance. The belief that faeries were elementals – creatures made only of earth, air, fire or water – seems to have been common among medieval magicians, who devised complex spells and rituals for raising them and using their powers. One such ritual, recorded in an early 15th century manuscript is now in the Bodleian Library in Oxford.

The underlying warning in British folklore, however, is that even the kindest of the Faere Folk are dangerous!

Summary

The faerie race that at one time inhabited Europe has left few traces, but it has survived in innumerable stories of elves and the Faere Folk. Many of the traditions associated with faeries are uniquely British, and one explanation is that they may have evolved from far-off memories of a Stone Age race that once lived in these islands. When the Celtic invaders from central Europe arrived in 500BC, they drove the original inhabitants into hiding in remote hills and caves.

It may well have seemed to the conquerors that there was an uncanny quality in the people they had displaced – the monuments they left behind would support this belief – they were small and dark; they lived underground; they were a secret people whose skill at hiding in the woods seemed to give them the power of invisibility. Long after the race had 'disappeared', or become absorbed into the population, the memory of these characteristics lived on in the Celtic tales about the indigenous people.

Nevertheless, one persistent story is that of the Physicians of Myddfai, a medical dynasty that lasted for 500 years, and who were said to be descended from a faerie 'Lady of the Lake' from Llyn-y-Fan-Fach, high on the slopes of the Black Mountain. The sons became physicians to Lord Rhys Gryg of Llandovery and Dynever in the 12th century and there were numerous descendants who were doctors, the last dying in Aberystwyth around the end of the 19th century (*Physicians of Myddfai*, Dr Harold Selcon).

It may also explain the subtle differences between witches and cunning-folk, in that the 'darker' nature of Old Craft stemmed from the 'taint of faerie blood' and an inherited dislike and/or distrust of the human race; while cunning-folk used their natural abilities to combat the more malevolent aspects of some witchcraft for the benefit of their neighbours.

The Story So Far ...

All students of faerie lore recognise that there is a strong connexion between witches and faeries. Margaret Murray, writing in 1921, even suggests that the cult of the faerie or primitive race survived until less than 300 years ago, and that the people who practised it were known as witches. And it has always been widely believed that those of British Old Craft had faerie blood ... and that belief persists to the present day.

- This close connexion reveals the witches' belief in the superiority of the faeries to themselves in the matter of magic and healing powers.
- The old adage within traditional witchcraft that 'a witch is born, not made', is also coupled with the belief that true witches are 'tainted with faerie blood'.
- Traditional witchcraft is held to be a natural ability, but not necessarily a hereditary one.

And if all this sounds too preposterous – that witches of a much later time carried the blood of a pre-Celtic people of these islands in their genes – then we must turn to the findings of science and Bryan Sykes, Professor of Human Genetics at the University of Oxford, who discovered that traceable DNA *could* survive for countless generations. In his book, *The Seven Daughters of Eve*, Professor Sykes compared the DNA taken from the body of the famous Iceman, discovered in the high Alps in 1991 with samples stored in the laboratory at Oxford – and found *an exact match* with a woman living in Dorset, England. 'There had to be an unbroken genetic link between [....] and the Iceman's mother, stretching back over 5,000-years and faithfully recorded in the DNA.'

And this wasn't the only example:

The remains from Gough's Cave (mentioned in an earlier chapter) were excavated in 1986 and now housed in the Natural History Museum, London. A DNA sample taken from Cheddar Man was compared with that of a local aristocrat, Alexander Thynn, Lord Bath, to see if they were related. The results showed that they were not; but Lord Bath's butler *was an exact match*. 'At a stroke he could claim an ancestry which stretched back 9,000-years, making the 500-year pedigree of the Thynns look distinctly nouveau,' wrote Professor Sykes.

As we can see from this scientific data, it *is* possible for DNA to extend back as far as the Collective Unconscious – but it doesn't mean that those carrying it will necessarily have inherited the ancestral attributes or natural abilities of their forebears!

Chapter Six

Black Angels (The Devil's Brood)

It's a funny thing – the past. Maybe there isn't really any past.
Maybe it's all back there waiting for you to find it ...
John P Marquand

The medieval period of English history was dominated by an Anglo-French ruling family, the Plantagenets – who gave England some of its most turbulent and colourful history. The men were warriors – ambitious, violent and brave – who were active Crusaders; while the women were even more terrifying!

The Plantagenets were descended from Mélusine, a mysterious maiden who married an Angevin noble, on the promise that he would never attempt to see her on a Saturday. Curiosity got the better of him and, concealing himself in her boudoir, discovered that from the waist down his wife had taken on the form of a serpent; she vanished into thin air but her spirit continued to haunt the castle, freezing the blood of the inhabitants with the sound of her cries. Another Angevin witch-countess was forced to go to mass by four of her husband's knights. She also disappeared without trace, at the consecration, leaving them holding the corners of her outer robe, from which came a strong odour of brimstone.

The Plantagenets probably revelled in their unsavoury reputation and were often referred to as 'the Devil's Brood' but according to Thomas B Costain in *The Pageant of England*, the 'English people were so proud of them that they forgave their wickedness and their peccadilloes'. Nevertheless, the legend was resurrected at the coronation of Richard I (1189), when a bat found its way into the Abbey and flew around during the ceremony, showing a preference for circling the coronation chair.

Still more alarming was a loud peal from the bell tower at the conclusion, compounding the belief that the date 3rd September was a day of ill-omen according to the astrologers.

The day prior to the coronation, Richard had issued a proclamation forbidding the attendance of Jews and witches at the ceremony [*The Conquering Family*, Thomas B Costain]. Tavern gossip of the time suggested that the reason why witches were included in the prohibition was because the King remembered his great-grandmother had flown out of the window of a church when confronted by the trappings of holiness! This, of course, is an over simplification, but if it was necessary to issue a proclamation citing the growing Jewish community, there must have been a significant number of witches around, too – because as we noted in an earlier chapter, you don't legislate against something that doesn't exist! Nothing, however, affected Richard Coeur de Lion's determination to go off on his Crusading adventures ...

Ironically, the most significant addition to medieval magic and medicine came about *as a result* of the Crusades – the First Crusade, following Pope Urban II's call in 1095, convinced 100,000 people to march for years across Europe, living off the land, to reclaim Jerusalem. Despite the 'orgy of violence' that horrified the Islamic world, many of the Crusaders carved out their own little empires along the way, demonstrating that different cultures living alongside each other can always make unexpected liaisons. Arabic learning in the fields of science, mathematics and medicine were absorbed by the invaders from all social and intellectual levels and, on returning home, they brought these newly acquired 'skills' with them – introducing Middle Eastern magic and healing to Britain. Ellis Peter's fictional character *Brother Cadfael* was based on this influx of learning.

Robert Graves (in his entry on modern witchcraft included in *The Necromancers*), also draws attention to the influences of an imported Saracen cult that was grafted onto local pagan stock. According to Graves, when the Saracens/Moors invaded Europe and seized Spain in 711 (soon controlling southern France, Savoy, Piedmont and part of Switzerland), they brought with them their own magico-mystic cults, whose rites consisted of 'ecstatic dancing, miraculous cures, and the pursuit of wisdom personified as a divine woman'.

The overview of medieval religion of the time reveals that it was still a great seasonal cycle of agricultural festivals, ritual observance and symbolic gesture from those earlier pagan celebrations that had been absorbed into the Church calendar. This was because the village or urban community's most usual gathering place, the local church, played host to many functions not envisioned by clerical direction. In *The Stripping of the Altars*, Eamon Duffy reveals that young men went to church to survey the young women, and one neighbour attempted to seduce another 'as they both went into evensong on the patronal festival of their parish church'.

Other occasions, such as St Agnes Eve, were less noted for their religious overtones than for the rituals by which young women hoped to divine the identity of their future lovers. According to Duffy, there were parish calendar days that hardly seemed religious at all. There were the 'hock' ceremonies, when bands of men and women held travellers of the opposite sex to ransom ... receiving some sanction from the clergy as the fines were used to augment church funds.

Plough ceremonies, held on the first working day after Christmas, were undisguised fertility rites, where young men from the villages harnessed themselves to a plough, which they dragged around the parish, ploughing up the ground in front of any household that refused to pay a token. 'Once again, these patently pagan observances were absorbed into the religious calendar; many churches had a 'plough-light' burning before the Sacrament or Rood,' writes Duffy.

Participation in church ceremonies was by no means an 'infallible indicator' of a person's piety or religious convictions. This idea is borne out by the fact that, even today, traditional Craft often retains the use of the Church calendar names for the major festivals – Candlemas, Roodmas, Lammas, Hallowmas – that has remained very much part of the agricultural year despite the repackaging.

It is not difficult to understand the relevance of the Church calendar, for there was no alternative, secular reckoning of time. The seasonal observances of the liturgical calendar affected everyone: legal deeds, anniversaries and birthdays were recorded by the religious festivals on which they occurred; while rents and leases fell on Lady Day, Lammas or Michaelmas. Medieval people, we are told, were fascinated by the passage of time for a variety of reasons: both practical and occult. Seed-time and harvest; when to gather acorns or to kill the pigs; the right time to let blood or take a laxative! All these were determined by the calendar. Many of the festivals still coincided with pagan festivals, or fell at key moments in the turning of the year at the summer and winter solstices: Our Lady's feast in harvest; the autumn festivals of the angels at Michaelmas, All Saints and All Souls at the change from autumn to winter, and so on.

Men and women who were not particularly devout, and who could not read, remembered the saints' days and other festivals by the Church calendar, but the outcome of all this was that the close interweaving of this calendar incorporated divisions that had little to do with the Christian year. Astrological patterns and the theme of the ages of man or the labours of the month became woven into religious primers, not only with the emblem of the saints whose feasts occurred then, but with a picture of the secular activities appropriate to that month.

We must also remember that the concept of witchcraft in Anglo-Saxon and Medieval England differed considerably from the hysteria that surrounded the later Tudor-Stuart 'burning times', and the happenings in continental Europe. Up to c1500, English witchcraft was viewed as damage to crops or livestock by spells or poison; or to people, ranging from sickness and sterility to death. The crime was not considered serious – it was a crime against a neighbour, rather than heresy, which was a crime against God – and the penalties tended to be like those for any other anti-social act. Conviction carried a relatively light punishment and few suffered death, unless they had caused the death of another human being. As late as 1467 (by which time thousands of heretics had already been burned in France), a convicted diviner trying to help locate thieves by the means of scrying, merely had to appear in public with a scroll on his head as a penance!

Across the Channel, things were *completely* different. Inspired by the fanatical teaching of the Spaniard, Dominic de Guzman, and his rabid hatred of heresy, in 1233 the Dominican Order's most infamous offspring was unleashed on an unsuspecting Europe – the Holy Inquisition. The Inquisition was a shock force of ecclesiastical butchers, but prior to its inauguration, the first to fall foul of the ignominious Dominicans were the Cathars of the Languedoc area of France.

The Cathars accepted reincarnation and sought religious or mystical experiences at first hand, not through the offices of an intermediary, i.e. the priesthood. They accepted the two irreconcilable principles of lightness and dark, spirit and matter, good and evil; recognising two gods – one being of pure spirit and unsullied by the taint of matter, the other of material creation. In saying that the world itself was intrinsically evil, in the eyes of Rome, the Cathars were guilty of a supreme heresy in regarding the material creation (for which Christ had died) as evil.

By 1200 there was also the fear that this particular brand of heresy could displace the Catholic Church, and so Rome decided to eliminate the opposition. In 1209, an army of 30,000 knights and foot-soldiers swept into the Languedoc and the Albigensian Crusades began. The whole area was devastated and in Beziers alone, over 15,000 men, women and children were slaughtered.

The hatred of de Guzman probably stemmed from his failure to convert the so-called heretics to the Catholic faith during his own zealous preaching in the area in 1204. By 1215, the Fourth Lateran Council decreed the total extermination of the Cathars (together with the Waldenses), on the charge of heresy. These atrocities lasted for nearly 40 years, culminating in the famous Siege of Montségur, which finally fell after ten months of heroic defiance by the townspeople.

De Guzman died in 1221, two years before the inauguration of the Inquisition, but the thirst for blood and searching out of heresy spurred the Dominicans on to greater refinements of brutal torture and execution. This time the target was the powerful and wealthy Order of the Poor Knights of Christ and the Temple of Solomon – or as they are more popularly known: the Knights Templar. The Order had had its roots in the Holy Land since 1118 and had gathered immense wealth from initiates, and even greater international power as a result of being involved in matters of high-level diplomacy.

By 1306 Philippe of France had decided to rid himself of the Templars, but due to the fact that they were a highly trained, professional military force much stronger than his own soldiers, he was unwilling to expel them by force. Also, Philippe had his eye on the Templar's wealth and was not about to let it slip through his fingers. At dawn on Friday 13th October, all Templars in France were arrested and subsequently accused of heresy. The Dominicans were at the forefront of the proceedings, their black cowls and white robes already recognisable as the uniform of death throughout Europe. The Grand Master of the Templars, Jacques de Molay, was roasted to death over a slow fire. Many of the Templars fled to England (as had possibly many of the Cathars before them) as a place of relative safety – and brought their 'mysteries' with them.

Once a victim had been denounced to the Inquisition there was no escape and it became a convenient way of settling old scores. A confessed witch or heretic could implicate another by claiming to have seen the accused attending a sabbat, but even if the accused confessed immediately on arrest, it was still necessary for her to undergo the prescribed torture – in case her first confession was false! The Inquisitors would not be denied their sport. Similarly in many cases the clerks taking down the confessions did not even bother to record the routine questions, and as the majority of confessions followed the same general pattern, their repetitiveness was held up as solid proof of the existence of witchcraft.

The content of the confessions, suggested by the Inquisitors and eagerly admitted to by the victims under torture, were the fantasies of the Inquisition, not of the unfortunate women, who hoped that by confessing the pain would cease and they would at least be strangled, rather than burned alive. Informing on neighbours was encouraged and it was unnecessary for the informer to openly confront the accused. A man or woman could be denounced to the Inquisition without knowing who the accuser was, or even on what evidence they had been arrested. Once accused the victim had no rights; witnesses were not identified; and often their accusations were not even made known to the defendant. No witnesses were allowed to testify on behalf of the accused, who was permitted no counsel, since the lawyer would be guilty of defending heresy.

England up to this period was fortunate in escaping much of this barbarism and hysteria that threatened to envelope Europe. The concept of witchcraft in the Middle Ages was one of almost benign acceptance in comparison with the later 16th-17th century 'conspiracies to overthrow the Christian God and trafficking with the Devil'. Local witches (or cunning folk) were still consulted on matters of medicine and healing, and it was only when they used their powers to the detriment of their neighbours that the law stepped in. And since legend claimed that the Plantagenets themselves were descended from the sorceress Mélusine, it was hardly likely that they were going to get themselves into a lather over the prospect of accusations of witchcraft, except to use it as a political weapon against one another. Between them they probably committed every crime in the book but they had one advantage over other European ruling houses – they were not slaves to Rome.

After the first excommunication, the ruling family and nobles became rather blasé over papal threats and tended to ignore them. Henry II had come in for some papal flack during the Becket affair (in which Thomas Becket, Archbishop of Canterbury, was murdered by some of the king's followers), but it was his son John who managed to get the whole of England excommunicated for disobeying the edicts of Innocent III. In *The Pageant of England,* Costain tells us that 'bans of excommunication which were hurled about in those days as freely as maledictions, flew back and forth ...' while Smith Minor observed that 'the Pope made a law that no one might be born, get married or die, for the space of ten years'. The English appear to have managed quite well without the offices of the Church of Rome, which suggests that many might, at this crucial time, have returned to their inherent paganism for spiritual comfort.

In fact, so tolerant were the Plantagenets of witchcraft that claims have been made that one of the highest Orders in the land, The Order of the Garter, stems from Edward III's quick-witted defence of his mistress, who had dropped her garter while dancing with the King. It has been suggested that the garter was a badge of membership of the witch-cult and by the King placing the garter on his own leg, he effectively silenced the nobles and clergy who would have accused the Countess of Salisbury of being a witch.

Upon examination the legend is not quite so preposterous as one might first think. Plantagenet ladies were not the shrinking violets that medieval ballads made them out to be and it would take considerably more than a falling garter to raise a blush.

Historian Thomas Beaumont James even commented that only at the instigation of a king as powerful as Edward III could such a famous order of chivalry have as its symbol an article of ladies' underwear! So the Countess of Salisbury's garter must indeed have conveyed some significant message to the onlookers. It has also been claimed that the Black Book containing the original constitution of the Garter disappeared after Edward's death. Whether there is any truth in such stories will never be known, but it is the stuff of which legends are made – **and a garter made of snake or hare's skin remains a badge of rank with traditional British Old Craft to the present day.**

As W E Hampton observes in his article 'Witchcraft and the Sons of York' published in *The Ricardian*: 'Students of the Wars of the Roses should note that accusations of witchcraft and sorcery were levelled, at times successfully, in every reign, whether of York or Lancaster, against members of the ruling royal family. Two of York's surviving sons made accusations of witchcraft against each other. The third, Richard of Gloucester, levelled accusations against the wife, the mother-in-law and mistress of his brother Edward ...'

In 1441 Eleanor Cobham, Duchess of Gloucester, was accused of having resorted to sorcery and witchcraft in order to destroy the King and advance her husband to the crown. Duke Humphrey had not been a popular figure during his brother Henry V's reign, and the accusations were politically motivated to discredit both the Duke and Duchess. So heavily did Duke Humphrey's enemies align themselves against the pair that Eleanor Cobham admitted most of the charges and was sentenced to public penance and perpetual imprisonment. (Neither did the Tudors hesitate to use the charge which Henry VIII used to destroy the most eminent of those Plantagenet descended nobles whose very existence the Tudors so resented).

It was around this time that proceedings of the sabbat began to appear in writing, but the details varied in detail according to period, nation or district, even social class and temperament. By the 16th century, however, apart from riding to the sabbat on goats or broomsticks, etc., the rites included trampling the cross underfoot; kissing the Devil's private parts behind in submission and homage; dancing in circles back to back and always treading to the left (an important part of the ceremony); parodying the mass and the liturgy burlesqued (all reminiscent of the ceremonies for which the Templars had suffered) ... 'The queen of the Sabbath [sic], the witch ranking first after the local 'Master', was usually the most experienced of the ladies. The local 'experts' would arrive to the number of thirteen, the 'master' and twelve subordinates, forming a 'coven'.' This is account was given by Montague Summers in his *History of Witchcraft*, but as Summers was a self-proclaimed priest and notoriously anti-pagan, his writing is extremely suspect.

Having said that, as a sceptical Reginald Scott in his *The Discoverie of Witchcraft* (1584) observed, some of the alleged cases of possession were faked – 'Lecherie covered with the cloak of witchecraft' – and many were drawn to these 'coarsely orgiastic rites believing that thus carnal satisfaction could be obtained without delay, and with a greater number than otherwise likely'. 'Witchcraft and the Sons of York' is another illuminating document in which W. E. Hampton cited the various incidents involving charges of witchcraft during that period. This quasi-legal method of upsetting a rival's apple-cart was used in much the same way as political scandal-mongering is used today. Love potions and poisons were among the magical remedies most in demand in both the French and English courts, and there are numerous recorded cases during this period that accuse members of the nobility of witchcraft.

The Christian calendar still strongly related to the turning points of the seasons – Christmas and the Winter Solstice; Easter and the Spring Equinox – which meant that although many observances associated with the religious celebrations were not exclusively Christian, they could easily be accommodated within a Christian framework. The dances and games associated with Easter, sometimes taking place inside the church, were clearly related to the spring theme of fertility. While the blessing of the candles at Candlemas represented the appearance of divine light in the darkness, or renewal and rebirth in the dead time of the year. People took the blessed candles away from the ceremony to be lit during thunderstorms, or in times of sickness, and to be placed in the hands of the dying. The following has more of a sense of spell or charm about it than a prayer:

> Whose candelle burneth cleere and bright, a wondrous force and
> might,
> Doth in these candles lie, which, if at any time they light,
> They sure believe that neither storm nor tempest dare abide,
> Nor thunder in the skie be heard, nor any divil spide,
> Nor fearfull sprites that walk by night, nor hurt by frost and haile.

Needless to say, the clergy were often nervous of such 'custom of folk' since it was believed that witches were 'capable of diverting such sacraments to nefarious ends': by dropping wax from a holy candle into the footprints of someone they hated, causing the victim's feet to rot off! It has also been suggested that so powerful was the lure of the female pagan elements, that in England during the mid 1300s, special prominence was given to the Virgin Mary, who became more and more important in the popular devotions of the late Middle Ages, as is demonstrated by the art of the time. Was this a conscious move by the Church to elevate Mary to rival the 'goddess' in the minds of the people? Nearly all the important pagan festivals had been incorporated into the Church calendar, so why should the clergy be above exchanging the Earth Mother for Mary, the Mother of God? How many old churches contain a simple lady chapel to the side of the main altar? Mary was not divine and hardly warrants a separate altar, unless it was to offer an alternative Christian female image – and Mary was the only suitable female they had to hand to neutralise pagan influences.

The arrival of the Black Death, however, brought about irrevocable changes in the social structure of Europe as a whole, and was arguably a serious blow to the Catholic Church, resulting in widespread persecution of minorities (*Sex, Dissidence and Damnation*, Jeffrey Richards) including those suspected of witchcraft. The 'softly, softly chatchee monkey' technique of the early missionaries was replaced with a 'big boots and boxing gloves' approach that held anyone demonstrating any kind of difference from their neighbours could be held responsible for God's wrath. From now on there would be no compromise, and religious austerity became the order of the day as represented by the grim *memento mori* that dominate later medieval art, literature and architecture, 'which became saturated in images of pain and death'.

As Philip Ziegler points out in *The Black Death*, paradoxically, the decades that followed the plague years saw not only a decline in the prestige and spiritual authority of the Church, but also a growth in religious fervour. Since the plague recurred in cycles every five to ten years throughout the Middle Ages, Jeffrey Richards claims that the established Church, having already suffered a growing loss of prestige during the plague years: 'failed to meet the challenge … under the circumstances the people looked to themselves for spiritual deliverance'.

All over Europe, what Ziegler calls 'co-fraternities' grew out of the ashes – drawing strength from the discontent and disillusionment of the people at large. If people were turning to the new religious fanaticism of the break-away Christian orders, it may possibly have been the ideal opportunity for the formation of the early 'covens' catering for those families who had kept one foot in the pagan camp and who couldn't cope with the new Christian austerity measures. The old witch-families may now have opened their doors to like-minded souls who had nowhere else to turn. This is pure speculation, of course, but if the argument can be put forward for the inauguration of a new Christian sauce for the medieval goose, then the same can be claimed for the old pagan gander.

The idea can easily be dismissed as a flight of fancy, if it wasn't for the motifs in the great medieval cathedrals and churches reflecting so much pagan imagery. This had persisted in the Early English and Decorated architectural styles when the art of ornamentation reached its highest peak, and which signalled the start of an age of prosperity cut short by the Black Death in 1348. Here we find the Green Man imagery often outnumbering the Christ-figures; and the Sheela-na-gigs, carved representations of a squatting, naked woman exposing her genitals. Such figures appear in many old Irish church built before the 16th century, as well as in mainland Britain, although many were defaced or destroyed as a result of 19th century Victorian prudery.

Another re-occurring theme is the imagery of the three hares, chasing each other in a circle: each of the ears in the image is shared between two animals, so that there are only three ears shown in total. In Devon there are 17 parish church containing roof bosses with this motif; in a chapel in Cotehele, Cornwall; in medieval stained glass in the Holy Trinity church in Long Melford, Suffolk; in a plaster church ceiling in Scarborough; on floor tiles in Chester Cathedral; in St David's Cathedral in Wales; and in the parish church in Long Crendon, Buckinghamshire. There are also instances of such images occurring in churches, chapels and cathedrals in France and Germany, as well as the Near and Far East.

All art of the time was sacred, 'with the purpose of presenting on earth a prefiguration of the realities which would be revealed to all humanity once it had passed over into death ...' writes Sir Roy Strong in *The Spirit of Britain*. So why were Dark and Middle

Age masons casting in stone for eternity the very images that were anathema to the Church? Stonemasons were among the elite craftsmen of the day – so no simple peasant beliefs for them. Was there some early tradition that required these images to be preserved under the trappings of Christianity, and which later evolved into the esoteric societies of the 16th and 17th centuries?

At this stage we should also pay some attention to the use of magic in medieval Britain for it was not only local 'wise women' who practised the art of healing. Professor Kieckhefer claims that necromancy was a fairly common indulgence of those in the lower holy offices. Education was not for the poor and most young men attending medieval universities would automatically be ordained to the lower orders, thereby qualifying as an exorcist and receiving at the ceremony of ordination an exorcist's bible as a symbol of office. And since many of the intelligentsia's notions of magic came from classical Graeco-Roman literature, a great deal of personal interest in the occult could be cloaked with an aura of academic respectability.

Kieckhefer also suggests that if bored young monks could engage in necromancy, so too might priests and friars, for the common denominator between them all was a basic knowledge of the rites of exorcism, in addition to a passing acquaintance with astrology, a classical education and many other forms of magic. The professor cites recorded cases of such men having access to infamous books on necromancy and, curious enough to try them out, being sternly chastised by their superiors. *Magic in the Middle Ages* illustrates just how extensively magic was used in medieval times. Kieckhefer is not preparing a case for or against the existence of witchcraft, but investigating the use of magic and the attitude to the practitioners of it during that formative period of our history. He sees magic of the medieval period as a historical intersection between religion and science, and whereas demonic magic invokes evil resting on a 'network of religious beliefs and practices, natural magic exploits occult powers within nature and is essentially a branch of medieval science'. It was during this period that medicine also began to evolve as an independent science, although many of the cures still smacked of sorcery, and in setting up their infirmaries, the monks absorbed remedies from classical sources as well as traditional local methods. There were still many types of unofficial healers, including midwives, and A. R. Myers *(England in the Late Middle Ages)* observes that when peasants fell ill, they relied chiefly on 'local women wise in the lore of herbs and other traditional remedies'. However, as the unprofessional rivals were always close to hand, the qualified physicians had every opportunity to cast the blame for their failures on the local witch, thereby removing the opposition. This was all too readily accepted, as throughout history, stories of magic and poison have gone hand in hand.

Summary

If we read between the lines, we can begin to see where witchcraft *might* have begun to develop into a more formal system. Although the common people were uneducated there were large numbers of the peasant classes who had followed their lords on a Crusade. Many perished along the way, but there would have been those returning who brought back some of the 'wisdom of the East'.

In addition, there was a large-scale movement of skilled workers due to the 'great cathedral race', the building fever that enveloped Europe – and which elevated the stonemasons to a unique social position with their knowledge of sacred geometry and labyrinth construction. 'Schemes of this kind pre-suppose a reasoned belief in the virtue of numbers, and in fact the Middle Ages never doubted that numbers are endowed with some occult power ... The divine wisdom is reflected in the numbers impressed on all things ... The construction of the physical and moral world alike is based on eternal numbers,' wrote Emile

Mâle in *The Gothic Image*. The 'treasure' of both the Templars and the Cathars has passed into legend – but what if these treasures were less temporal than of a mystical, esoteric kind?

Set in the huge undecorated floor of Chartres cathedral, for example, is the largest single decoration in the whole building: the labyrinth, observes Colin Ward in *Chartres: The Making of a Miracle*:

> It is about twelve metres, or forty feet, in diameter, and the path of white stones, separated by thinner blue ones, to the centre is 294 metres long. Labyrinths like this were built in several of the French cathedrals, though only three remain ... as the authors of a monograph exploring the possible signifi-cance of the labyrinth at Chartres suggest, whatever its meaning and function was, it had been long forgotten by the eighteen century, which is remarkable since it must have been put in place for a significant reason 'taking up so much of one of the most sacred pieces of ground in European Christendom' ...

It took 40 years for the Albigensian Crusade to completely suppress the Cathars and it would not be unreasonable to presume that many of them *were* able to leave France, taking their concept of dualism with them. The Cathars believed that the material universe was created by an 'evil spirit' and that souls were the angels who fell from heaven, imprisoned in one body after another – yearning to escape from the material world and re-enter the heaven of pure spirituality (*Europe's Inner Demons*). Towards the close of the 12th century this interpretation was conveniently 'demonised' by a French monk, Rudolf Ardent, who claimed that the Cathars believed that 'whereas God created all invisible things, the Devil created all visible one; so they worshipped the Devil as the creator of their bodies'.

Similar charges were levelled at the Templars, accusing them of spitting or trampling on a crucifix, 'the kiss of shame', dancing back to back, worshipping idols, etc., although as Norman Cohn observes, the charges against them were absolutely without foundation. The Inquisition's 'Devil' in this case appears to be founded on the image of Baphomet – a vague description that was later interpreted by Eliphas Levi (19th century) as the duality of male and female, heaven and earth, night and day, signified by the raising of one arm and the downward gesture of the other – or 'any of the major harmonious dichotomies of the cosmos'. As Professor Norman Cohn observes:

There is in fact no serious evidence for the existence of such a sect of Devil-worshippers anywhere in medieval Europe. One can go further: there is serious evidence to the contrary ... To understand why the stereotype of a Devil-worshipping sect emerged at all, why it exercised such fascination and why it survived so long, one must look not at the belief or behaviour of heretics, Dualist, or other, but into the minds of the orthodox themselves. Many people, and particularly many priests and monks, were becoming more and more obsessed by the overwhelming power of the Devil and his demons. That is why their idea of the absolute evil and anti-human came to include Devil-worship, alongside incest, infanticide and cannibalism.

Rome was now in the position of either having to operate in tandem with the many other minority groups springing into existence in medieval Europe, or suppress them by the process of complete annihilation. In *Sex, Dissidence and Damnation*, Jeffrey Richards presents an authoritative study of six medieval groups, which the Church broadly fitted into religious (Jews, witches, heretics) and sexual (homosexual, prostitutes and lepers) categories, with one common denominator – *perverted sex*.

It was this stereotype of the 'lustful deviant' closely linked with the Devil that was used to demonize them all, and to be identified by the Church as being part of a worldwide satanic conspiracy aimed at undermining Christianity in the 11th century. During the Middle Ages there was a deep entrenchment of an alternative morality to that required by the clergy, which Richards identifies as a morality of pre-Christian tribal and peasant society, in which sexual life was unrestricted by religious dogma. Marriages of the time were often informal affairs and easily dissolved; and if the sexual act was believed to be innocent and pleasure derived from it, then it was not disagreeable to God.

Needless to say, these pagan attitudes were anathema to the Church, which associated all illicit sex with the Devil and subsequently there were certain elements of paganism that defied Christian absorption, particularly the fertility cults. In Richards' opinion, overt paganism with its strong overtones of magic continued to exist and to be fought by the Church and State until the 9th century. Indeed early medieval laws contain regular references to witchcraft, though not, as Richards' points out, as Devil-worship.

Seen in its true perspective, it is possible to trace the Christian allegations made against witches and heretics as being exactly the same as those made by classical writers against the early Christians – incest, infanticide, sodomy, cannibalism and orgies. In fact, according to medievalist Norman Cohn it was *standard practice* to brand all dissident religious groups with the most heinous of crimes, and by the Middle Ages a common stock of slanders existed in the classical texts for the monastic writers to plunder and redeploy. Such texts were regularly lifted verbatim and applied to the new dissident groups.

Professor Cohn also explains that early Christian writers took this familiar propaganda technique further– thereby creating a convincing but deceptive image of an overall satanic conspiracy. It is his contention that Devil-worshipping witches had no existence in popular culture, indeed no existence at all outside the fevered imaginations and paranoid delusions of a group of medieval clerical intellectuals. He also traces the development of the 'satanic witch-cult' in the cumulative process of propaganda by which all religious dissidents were demonised, and its irony lies in that many of the heretical groups branded as Devil-worshippers were more pious and chaste than their accusers.

Once this pattern of satanic activities was established as part of the propaganda machine, it could be regularly amended and extended to include any other unspeakable acts that came to light in classical sources. The recurrence of the same ideas in the accounts of the persecutions of the Jews, Waldenses, Cathars and the Knights Templar all demonstrate identical allegations of Devil worship and sodomy, which became synonymous with all forms of lechery, sexual deviance, leprosy and magic. Evidence was usually given of the licentious heretical practices which involved kissing the Devil under his tail – the kiss of shame so vividly described during later proceedings at a Scottish trial, when one of the accused claimed that: 'The Devil caused all the company to come and kiss his arse, which they all said was cold like ice.' This obscene kiss featured among the accusations levelled at both the Waldenses and the Knights Templar, although Michael Howard has never heard of its use within modern witchcraft, despite fictional accounts so frequently quoted. It also was around this period that tales began to spread of the Jewish community condoning the ritual murder of Christian children as part of their rites.

Although the Church pursued witches as heretics from the 9th century, the witch-trials on a grand scale happened after 1300. Jeffrey Richards suggests that these can be linked to the climatic change in Europe around that time which unleashed a succession of harvest failures, floods, famines and plagues. The cause of this was blamed on witches and heretics who had brought the wrath of God down on the populace, with their guilt only able to be expunged by casting them into the flames. Added to the various political scenarios that existed at the time, and finding it expedient to remove such opposition as the Cathars and Templars, the Church subjected Europe to an ecclesiastical spring clean.

Richards concludes his chapter on witches by conclusively rejecting the idea that Devil-worshipping witches really existed, and that those who continued to follow the old pagan traditions were targeted as unholy conspirators. 'There may have been a few stray eccentrics who did worship the Devil but the satanic conspiracy was the creation of Catholic intellectuals, theologians, and jurists who merged ancient folk beliefs, learned magic, and rural witchcraft, emphasised the role of sex and postulated the aim of destroying Christendom.' The satanic witches of the late Middle Ages were, then, the ultimate scapegoats, an invented minority, a composite image of evil, ready-made for application to anyone who disagreed with Church dogma, which was fed into the public consciousness until it bore horrific fruit in the later witch hunts of the 16th and 17th centuries.

Adding fuel to the growing satanic conspiracy propaganda, the Dominican, Thomas Aquinas (1227-74), penned *Quaestiones Quodlibetales*, which influenced ecclesiastical thinking on witchcraft of that period and laid the foundation for the ensuing persecutions. Even as late at 1879, Pope Leo XIII decreed that all Catholic clergy should 'take the teachings of Aquinas as the basis of their theological position' and Sprenger and Kramer, co-authors of the *Malleus Maleficarum*, quoted him as one of their principle authorities. Aquinas too, seems to have been preoccupied with the sexual habits of the Devil and, according to his reasoning, what a demon was capable of doing with stolen semen as a means of artificial insemination would be the envy of any modern fertility clinic!

The witch-persecutions that engulfed Europe for almost 500 years were the product of religious hysteria, born out of the fear of competition. The Christian Devil had been created for them out of Old Testament translations; he could be identified with the horned deities of older religions and since the female aspect of the Goddess reflected Rome's dislike of, and belief in, the corrupting influence of women, it was easy to pronounce witchcraft as being Devil infested.

The most excessive example of this attitude is to be found in the most damning of all works on witchcraft – *Malleus Maleficarum (The Hammer of Witches)*, first published in 1486, which ran into 14 editions during the next 40 years. Although it has long been accepted that there is not one grain of truth in it, this perverted brainchild of two more Dominicans, Jacobus Sprenger and Heinrich Kramer, became the irrefutable Papal approved gospel of execution and torture throughout Europe, ultimately claiming an estimated figure that could rival the Holocaust of the 20th century. Jeffrey Richards defines it as a work of 'pathological misogynism and sex-obsession'.

The Folio version used for this text is based on the translation by the Rev. Montague Summers (hence his reputation as an expert on modern witchcraft), with an introduction by Pennethorne Hughes who describes it as 'a textbook of procedure: an official blueprint for the suppression of an underground movement against the Christian structure of medieval society ... Extermination must be careful but ruthless ... together with the means to extract confession and effect punishment. It expressed terror and authorised extermination.'

The *Malleus Maleficarum* in its original form makes for difficult reading and Hughes shies away from including passages of the tortures and executions, by claiming that such 'details of human torture and degradation are best confined to medical textbooks and under-the-counter sadism'. Even in its abridged form, however, the Folio edition still gives a good indication of the Dominicans' preoccupation with sexual matters. Their fiction of sexual encounters with demons and incubi, and the methods of exacting confessions from their victims, rank with the rather excessive fantasies and sado-masochistic daydreams of de Sade rather than what we would expect from holy law.

The Story So Far ...

Did an embryonic grouping of like-minded people grow out of a rural community's need for company and companionship in the dark days during and following the plague-years? That question arises especially if the local cunning folk remained to help cure the sick when the clergy had all but fled. New methods of healing and the introduction of exotic perfumed herbs coming in from Europe and the Middle East would have increased the kudos of the community witches (and cunning folk) – and the traditional methods of healing *were* attracting the attention of the local monks, who were frantically compiling the herbals we are familiar with today. As we are also aware, the Plantagenet family were not slaves to Papal doctrine and as early as 1279 Edward I forbade the grants of land to the Church – in the Statute of Mortmain – the first act of anti-clerical legislation in England (*The Medieval World 800-1491*). Those branded 'heretic' in the eyes of the Inquisition often found sanctuary on English soil, despite the threats of excommunication and exhortation to hand over the 'guilty' for punishment.

Anyone and everyone it seems had access to magic, and in *Magic in the Middle Ages* we can also see how magic, blending primitive folklore with the academic learning pouring in from the Middle East, herbal remedies and thaumaturgic healing, became the province of peasant and educated alike – often with a cross-pollination of ideas between the higher and lower levels of intellect. And if exhortation to God did not heal the sick, then the people turned back to the old ways and consulted the local wise woman for a cure. As we know, it was not unknown for witch-craft to be used while invoking the assistance of some Christian saint, as is shown in the texts of the books of household management faithfully recorded in the Wolfsthurn and Munich handbooks.

According to *Grimoires: A History of Magic Books*, there is ample evidence that the medieval clergy were the main practitioners of ritual or ceremonial magic and therefore the owners, transcribers and circulators of *grimoires*, while several were attributed to various popes. Owen Davies shows that 'with the increased contact between Christians, Hebrews and Muslims through the Crusades and the Moorish occupation of Spain, various magical ideas and concepts originating in the Islamic world, found their way into European *grimoires*'. The most famous of these were the Arabic 13th century *Picatrix* and *Book of Honorius*, and the 15th century Hebrew *Lesser Key of Solomon the King* – still popular with ritual magicians today.

Access to books on magic and mysticism, as well as the exotic strangers claiming sanctuary in England, all helped fuel the interest in occult subjects; and *grimoires* became the medieval version of the 'best-sellers'. There would also be a blend of traditional magic with the more ceremonial approach demanded by the Catholic Church, and so familiar modern rites and rituals possibly have their roots in this medieval, magico-religious melting-pot. Old Craft in its purest form would probably have been almost extinct except for remote rural pockets where the flame would have often struggled to survive – except that the wearing of a snakeskin garter as a badge of rank is still extant in contemporary Old Craft circles.

Chapter Seven

Eleven Echoes of Autumn
(Elizabethan England)

In any age of any society the study of history, like other social activities, is governed by the dominant tendencies of the time and place.
Arnold Toynbee, *A Study of History*

Paradoxically, although it was during the Elizabethan era that the hysteria surrounding witchcraft began gathering momentum in England and Scotland, it was also a great time of occult learning among the intelligentsia. As we have seen, up until this time, the English attitude had been fairly ambivalent towards its witches and cunning folk.

In her book, *The Sociology of Health and Healing*, Professor Margaret Stacey is very conscious of both the curative powers and the important role played by healers and wise women, especially for poorer people living in the country. The people believed in a world full of 'power', for both good and evil. Historians also insist that this belief cannot be dismissed as delusion on the part of the uneducated; the belief in supernatural powers was shared by the highest and the lowest in the land and it took a variety of forms. 'Since it appears to have been fully credible to all the villagers, and to the presiding magistrates [at the witch trials of 1566 and 1576], who included the Queen's Attorney, Sir John Fortescue (later Chancellor of the Exchequer) and Thomas Cole, Archdeacon of Essex.'

This was not just a matter of continuing pagan belief, the Church still recognised the 'power' of healing, and had built up its own system 'which one can only describe as magical' inasmuch as it proclaimed saints, shrines and images to have healing properties. Needless to say, the church, jealously guarding its newly established position following the Reformation, did not approve of the powers attributed to cunning men and women, and was bitterly opposed to any who exercised powers other than those it had itself bestowed.

Although the cunning folk were in almost all cases Christian themselves, certain Christian theologians and Church authorities believed that, being practitioners of magic, the cunning folk were in league with the Devil, and as such were akin to the more overtly Satanic and malevolent witches. Partly due to this, laws were enacted across England, Scotland and Wales that often condemned cunning folk and their magical practices, but there was no widespread persecution of them akin to the witch hunt, largely because most common people firmly distinguished between the two: witches were seen as being harmful and cunning folk as useful.

Owen Davies, *Popular Magic: Cunning-Folk in English History*

Witch hunts were systematically mounted throughout Tudor and Stuart England but most witches, wise women and cunning folk called upon God or the saints: *'God bless; I touch; God heals'*. Other recorded healers, such as Margaret Hunt in the 1520s, instructed their patients to recite *"paternosters, Ave Marias* and creeds' repetitiously, and for a ritually defined number of times.

Pater Noster, Ave Maria, Criede,
Learn the childe yt is need.

When some healers were brought to trial they defended themselves by saying that they had not used 'powers' at all, they had simply used their empirical knowledge of healing, applying herbs and the like.

Drawn from books of advice, memoirs and records from the big houses of the time, a later *Working Life of Women in the 17th Century*, reveals that what we would call 'domestic plant medicine' was now commonplace. Girls learned from their mothers, as had their mothers before them – from the humble housewives to the upper-class chatelaine, both exhibited similar 'empirical' knowledge and skills in healing. **Although it's possible that prayers, charms or spells were part of the treatment, these women were not witches.**

When the skills of the household were exhausted there *were* a variety of healers to be called upon – diviners, wise women and cunning folk – who continued to be important for the majority who lived in the country. During the 16th-17th centuries these popular healers went under a variety of names – cunning men, wise women, charmers, blessers, conjurors, sorcerers, witches – who offered a variety of services that ranged from healing sick animals and people to finding lost goods, fortune telling and divination of all kinds. It was a mixture of accumulated experience based on nursing and midwifery, combined with inherited lore about the healing properties of plants and minerals, but including ritual healing.

'Green' men and women had the right bestowed on them during the reign of Elizabeth I (the Wild Herb Act) to gather herbs and roots from wild, uncultivated land – but it was an occupation that had been going strong since the late 14th century. A new kind of medical herbalist had evolved – the apothecary – who purchased herbs collected from the countryside by these wandering herb collectors. In *Green Pharmacy*, Barbara Griggs records that during the 17th century herbs could also be bought direct from the herb-women in Newgate Market or Covent Garden.

The theories of the Greek physician Galen were currently undergoing a great revival; these were based on the theory of 'humours', which involved notions of balance, especially between hot and cold, wet and dry. On the continent, Paracelsus also made contributions that were important in the development of pharmacology. He learned a great deal from indigenous traditions and cunning folk about the properties of herbal medicine, and he replaced the traditional pharmacopoeia with what he had discovered. As a result, from 1640, Paracelsus became a dominant influence in English medicine.

Alchemy was also experiencing a revival in the 16th century. The writings of the 13th century Franciscan monk, Roger Bacon, known as Doctor Mirabilis, was the major authority and alchemy was a compulsive interest in court circles. Alchemy, which was associated with the mythological traditions of ancient Greece and Arabia, played a unifying role in drawing upon the skills of linguists, scholars, mathematicians and natural philosophers. According to Diana Fernando, 'Alchemy is one of the four esoteric paths to enlightenment, along with Magia, astrology and Kabbalah.' The magical encyclopaedia *Man, Myth & Magic* tells us that it was 'more an art than a science and its most important and most interesting aim was the spiritual transformation of the alchemist himself.'

The men who followed this path were well versed in the languages of magic and mystery: Latin, Hebrew and Greek – and the most famous of all was John Dee. In the eyes of his contemporaries he was a charlatan, impostor and dabbler in black magic; from a historical perspective he was one of the most remarkable of Elizabethan scholars, a noted scientist, an authority on mathematics, navigation and astronomy – as well as being Astrologer Royal to Elizabeth I. He was also employed in the Queen's secret service, and how far his magical activities were a cover for espionage is a question that remains unsolved to this day.

In partnership with a rather dubious medium Edward Talbot (afterwards Kelly), John Dee embarked on a series of experiments with crystals and shew-stones (two of which are now in the British Museum) to communicate with 'angels' as a means of acquiring universal knowledge. According to Dee these were 'intelligent beings, telepathically attuned to a knowledge of the past and future'. These 'angelic conversations' were dictated to Kelly in the angel's own language, called Enochian – the 'calls' being part natural magic, part mathematical, part pure cryptography. Needless to say, Dee has his detractors, but some 500 years later we find Aleister Crowley writing extensively in his Confessions about the magical authenticity of the Keys. What we must also bear in mind is that what Dee referred to as 'angels' could not appear as anything else to his Christian mindset.

According to Kurt Seligmann's *The History of Magic*, among the English Qabbalists the greatest one and perhaps the only one who grasped the ensemble of the doctrine was Robert Fludd (1574-1637). The Qabbalah is a metaphysical or mystical system and Fludd discovered this while writing his *History of the Macrocosm* in which he states that man is a miniature version (or microcosm), physically and spiritually of the universe (the macrocosm). He immediately rewrote his system, basing it on the teaching of the Rabbis, instead of on the classical philosophies, which, until then, had been his chief authorities. Fludd's influence is subtle rather than obvious and a large number of contemporary esoteric writers use his ideas, without realising the source is an obscure Elizabethan scholar!

This fascination of magic and alchemy can be gauged by the number of 16th and 17th century plays on the subject, such as Marlowe's *Dr Faustus*, Greene's *Friar Bacon and Friar Bungay* and Lyly's *Gallethea*. Shakespeare reflects in his plays the whole-hearted belief of the people at large in the existence of good and bad spirits. *Hamlet* and *Macbeth* were set against a background of witchcraft and the supernatural; his romances feature fairy beings in the wood near Athens (*Midsummer Night's Dream*) and the spirits that obeyed the commands of Prospero in *The Tempest*. All of these would have been as real to Shakespeare's audiences as the characters of Helena and Miranda. Ben Jonson gave us *The Alchemist, The Masque of Queens, Oberon: the Faery Prince* and *Mercury Vindicated from the Alchemists at Court.*

These plays were written for public entertainment but they were to have some serious repercussions in the years to come ...

Summary

In his famous *Encyclopedia of Witchcraft and Demonology,* Rossell Hope Robbins erroneously states that witchcraft came to England in 1563, but as we have seen, it was a continuance of something that had always been there, and was obviously still being practised strongly in rural districts. What Dr Robbins should have stated was that legalised witch-hunting came to England in 1563.

Under the Tudors the whole social and religious structure in England changed when Henry VIII brought about the dissolution of the monasteries, broke away from Rome and declared himself head of the Church of England. Strangely enough, although the people were no longer under allegiance to Rome, this period of history saw the start of the witch-trials in this country, which hitherto had escaped the horrors being enacted in Europe. Using witchcraft and heresy as an excuse, the Tudors climbed on the bandwagon of the trumped-up-charge to destroy the remaining Plantagenet descendents whose very existence they resented.

Anne Boleyn was accused of being a witch although she was executed for her alleged adultery; Mary burned a few heretics in an attempt to curry favour with Philip of Spain and get him into her bed; while Elizabeth removed a few more to put the Catholics back in their place and signed the Statute of 1563 resulting from 'pressure of the clergy and made the Devil an acknowledged factor in the laws of the state'.

With the accession of the House of Stuart to the throne (1603) open season was declared on practitioners of witchcraft. Fitting the mood of the times, Shakespeare's 'weird sisters' created an indelible caricature of witches, which has persisted in theatrical adaptations ever since. Taken at face value, the three witches are asked to do no more than divine Macbeth's bloodstained future, but the Bard added to the growing political, anti-witch hysteria by creating in his own inimitable fashion, that *pot-pourri* of fiendish horror with which we are all familiar. Although much in dispute, the date given for the first appearance of *the Scottish play* is generally thought to be 1605-6, some three years after Elizabeth's death, but the characterisation no doubt reflected the public image of witches as the 'secret, black and midnight hags' of the Elizabethan witch-trials that had taken place during the preceding 50 years.

Not so famous, but even nastier, were the characters created by Ben Jonson for his *Masque of Queens*. The masque was performed on 2nd February 1609 at Whitehall Palace, with costumes and a stage design by Inigo Jones in such a lavish production that its estimated cost was £1,400 for a single performance. The manuscript has survived intact, complete with Jonson's handwritten and elaborate stage settings, which was afterwards presented to Prince Henry. The theme of the masque was Evil being put to flight by Heroic Virtue; Jonson's reason for having an anti-masque featuring witches was due to James I having written a book on witchcraft and being obsessed by the subject. It does seem strange, however, that in a climate of witch-hysteria, a production such as *The Masque of Queens* should be staged for mere amusement. Unlike the rest of Europe, perhaps the English court felt itself immune from any danger and could afford to be amused by Jonson's unsavoury cast – comparable perhaps with today's alternative comedy extracting humour from terrorism. Those not affected by such happenings could afford to be smug at others' expense.

Although Robert Turner of Holshott lived after John Dee (who died in 1608) his translations helped to keep the Elizabethan hermetic tradition alive, long after the glory of the era had faded. Turner's translations of important magical and alchemical texts date from the 12th to the 15th and 16th centuries, including works by Paracelsus and Cornelius Agrippa. These works were highly influential in Elizabethan occult circles, although they were usually in Latin, and often only available in written form.

Turner's translations have never been surpassed, providing an insight into the magical world of the 16th century, not only for his contemporaries, but for occult researchers and magicians ever since – including Francis Barrett when he was compiling *The Magus* (1801) and A W Waite. It is important, however, to note the history of one of Turner's translations – *the Ars Notoria* – a magical process by which the magician could instantly gain knowledge or memory of all the arts and sciences.

The importance of the *Ars Notoria* has declined somewhat over the past two hundred years, owing to its association with the spurious grimoire of the *Lemegeton: The Lesser Key of Solomon*, a seventeenth-century compilation of five independent 'Solomonic' magical writings united by a descriptive title page. The *Lemegeton* consists of *Goetia: the Book of Evil Spirits, Theurgia-Goetia*, the *Pauline Art*, the *Art Almadel* and the *Ars Notoria*. It was probably compiled by an anonymous occultist who wished to assemble the lesser works attributed to Solomon into one convenient volume. Twentieth-century occultists, such as A W Waite, have seen fit to distort the facts surrounding the composition of the *Lemegeton*, extolling the work as a legendary grimoire and overlooking the earlier independent existence of its individual parts. The Elizabethan magi knew nothing of the *Lemegeton*, but they were familiar with the contents.
Robert Turner, *Elizabethan Magic*

Sadly, Robert Turner of Holshott's early death meant that he was unable to complete his plans for further translations, and as a result, these early manuscripts are now lost to occult researchers.

The Story So Far ...

The Elizabethan era witnessed the seeds being sown for the massive magical Renaissance due to bear fruit in the generations that followed. Learned men were collecting important manuscripts from Europe and the Middle East relating to magic, alchemy and the Qabbalah; and up until the Statute of 1563, no laws were on the statute books in England relating to witchcraft. It therefore seems ironic that the seeds were also being sown for the English witch-hunts, which up until then had escaped the Inquisitional frenzies that were going on across the Channel.

It is doubtful, however, whether the two factions were ever in a position to exchange ideas, unlike earlier times when local monks courted the wise women for their herbal knowledge. The embryonic components of what would later be referred to as ritual magic, were the province of the educated and titled; witchcraft remained a 'below stairs' activity – and in Elizabethan England, never the twain shall meet. There is no doubt that witchcraft *was* flourishing, although Shakespeare and Jonson were merely embellishing the gossip of the time for dramatic effect. In Jonson's case, however, he was pandering politically to the obsession of James I, who had written a book on witchcraft, *Daemonologie*, which reflected the popular *Scottish* views of the day.

It is also worth noting that both Shakespeare and Jonson feature Hecate as the principal of the group of witches, although according to *The Oxford Companion to Classical Literature*, she was a 'Greek goddess unknown to Homer, but according to Hesiod, she was great and beneficent deity in many departments of life, war, council, games, horsemanship, farming, etc.' She only later became the protectress of enchanters and witches, associated with the lower world and with night; transformed into a queen of ghosts and magic, haunting crossroads, attended by hell-hounds. In contemporary witchcraft, she is often identified as the 'Crone', although this conflicts with her characterisation as a virgin and occasionally as a mother in all classical and historical sources. The following is taken from a prayer addressed to Hecate taken from *Readings in Late Antiquity: A Sourcebook* – 'The queen of rites is Hecate, virgin goddess of the underworld ... 'Lady, earth-cleaver, leader of the hounds, subduer of all, worshipped in the streets, three-headed, light-bearing, august virgin ...''

Her role as a triple goddess has led to her being identified with the concept of 'Maiden, Mother and Crone', an interpretation made popular by Robert Graves in *The White Goddess* despite the fact that it has no obvious parallel in the ancient world according to *Virgin Mother Crone: Myths and Mysteries of the Triple Goddess*, by Donna Wilshire. This modern association is rooted in the 20th century with Aleister Crowley being one of the first to name her as a crone in his esoteric novel, *Moonchild (The Butterfly Net)*.

Any reference to the existence of covens from this time is also suspect. The word was originally a late medieval Scottish word (c1500) meaning a gathering of any kind, according to the *Oxford English Dictionary* and derives from the Latin root word *convenire* meaning 'to come together' or 'to gather', which also gave rise to the English word *convene*. The first recorded use of it being applied to witches comes much later, from 1662 in the witch-trial of Isobel Gowdie, which describes a coven of 13 members: although Jonson refers to a gathering of 11 witches and the Dame in *The Masque of Queens*.

The word 'coven' remained largely unused in English until 1921 when Margaret Murray promoted the idea in *The Witch-Cult in Western Europe*, but it is now hotly disputed that all witches across Europe met in groups of 13, which they called 'covens' – while the term 'sabbat' is of Hebrew origin, meaning 'to cease' or 'to rest'. Some allusions to meetings of witches with demons are also made in the *Malleus Maleficarum* (1486), but it was during the Renaissance when 'sabbat folklore' was most popular; more books on them were published, and more people lost their lives as a result.

Despite the numerous claims by the 'establishment' of the time concerning the witches' sabbat, modern research has been unable to find any corroboration that any such event ever occurred. Scott E. Hendrix in his study, *The Pursuit of Witches and the Sexual Discourse of the Sabbat,* presents a two-fold explanation for why these stories were so commonly told in spite of the fact that sabbats likely never actually occurred. Most importantly, the belief in the existence of witches was widespread in late medieval and Renaissance Europe. Secondly, the descriptions of the sabbats were published by priests, jurists and judges from transcriptions made during the process of the witchcraft trials. That these testimonies reflect actual events is for most of the accounts considered doubtful and Norman Cohn argues in *Europe's Inner Demons,* that they were 'determined largely by the expectations of the interrogators and free association on the part of the accused, and reflect only popular imagination of the times, influenced by ignorance, fear and religious intolerance towards minority groups'.

We should not, however, ignore Carlo Ginzburg's *Ecstasies: Deciphering the Witches' Sabbath,* reporting on his discovery of a group of individuals in northern Italy, calling themselves *benandanti,* who believed that they went out of their bodies in spirit and fought amongst the clouds against evil spirits to secure prosperity for their villages, or congregated at large feasts presided over by a goddess, where she taught them magic and performed divinations. Ginzberg acknowledged that **the participants themselves *knew* they were describing out-of-body, rather than physical, occurrences.** Between 1575 and 1675, in the midst of the witch trials the *benandanti* were tried as heretics under the Inquisition and their beliefs assimilated to satanism – which may have provided 'evidence' for the ongoing belief in the existence of the sabbat as part of the European witch-cult.

In the relative safety of England, witches obviously went about their business as solitaries, or as part of a family group, and as Robin Briggs states quite categorically in *Witches and Neighbours*: 'There is no good evidence that a single coven existed or that witches ever participated in a sabbat of any kind. The natural conclusion from the documentary sources is that the whole myth of the sabbat was a fabrication from beginning to end.'

Chapter Eight

Songs, Drones and Refrains of Death (The Burning Times)

On Sundays in the late 1620s, the village echoed to the sounds of music and dancing. In the mornings the parson would say common prayer briefly in the church ... and 'the rest of the day even till dark night almost, except eating time, was spent in dancing under a maypole and a great tree ... where all the town did meet together'.
Keith Wrightson, *English Society*

As Keith Wrightson, lecturer in Modern History at the University of St Andrews, points out in *English Society 1580-1680*, by 1580, England had been a Protestant kingdom for almost a generation. The Reformation had come about because Henry VIII wanted to marry Anne Boleyn and produce a legitimate heir to the English throne. Up to that point, English Catholicism (as we have seen) had co-existed quite harmoniously with the idiosyncrasies of incorporating pagan revelry and maintaining its medieval traditions.

The problem facing the new Anglican Church, was that it had not succeeded in altering the devotional habits of the common people. The new faith was one of learning, based on a specific theological belief, while uneducated folk still followed a religion that has been described as a 'system in ingrained observances'; their prayers more like spells and charms than devotion. Away from the main centres of reformation, even supposed Anglicans still insisted on traditional rituals at baptisms, weddings and funerals: there was also a continued reverence for ancient crosses, or even their sites, and 'burial parties on their way to the church might circle them sunwise before passing on their way'. In Cleveland it was reported in the 1580s that *'when any dieth, certaine women sing a song to the dead body, reciting the journey that the parte must go'* – doubtless the Lyke Wake Dirge, a song riddled with pagan imagery.

A stubborn attachment to these traditional rituals and obser-vances was not, in itself, a problem. What was a thorn in the flesh of the new clergy was the people's reluctance to put aside their dependence on supernatural agencies to protect against the dangers and misfortunes of a hostile environment, and the atten-tions of evil spirits. This attitude, as we have already discussed, existed quite happily within the medieval Church, where the accepted trafficking with supernatural powers could at best be described as magical, at worst foolish. For the Anglicans, however, whose doctrine preached that all happenings on earth, good or bad, came from an omnipotent God, alternative explana-tions of good and evil spirits, or the neglect of omens and obser-vances, were anathema.

Their 'new' Christian god was to be supplicated, not commanded – and to resort to witchcraft and counter-magic was to consort with the Devil! No matter how hard it tried, the clergy was constantly out-manoeuvred by a shadowy cast of astrologers, diviners, wise women and cunning folk. Villagers would travel miles to consult a respected cunning man, but would quickly baulk at the prospect of attending weekly divine service in bad weather. As Keith Wrightson says, the reason was simple enough:

> Magic catered for needs which were still felt, but which were no longer met by a 'purified' church. The strength and variety of magical belief of the time is recorded in the numerous records of witchcraft trials. Witchcraft in England was not primarily associated with the worship and service of the devil … the witchcraft statute of 1604 makes reference to the diabolical compact. The law was far more concerned with simple '*maleficium*', the power to do harm by use of unidentified

supernatural powers. The classic circumstances of a witchcraft accusation were those in which a quarrel between neighbours, often accompanied by threat and curses, was succeeded by the occurrence of an inexplicable misfortune.

There were many such accusations heard in the English courts. The peak of prosecutions was reached in the last two decades of the 16th century, and cases continued to be brought regularly in the first decade of the 17th century. Those accused were usually women, commonly old and often widows; almost invariably neighbours of their accusers, and were usually of lower social status than those persons they were alleged to have harmed.

In light of these facts, it seems probable that the rising tide of witchcraft accusations in the latter part of Elizabeth's reign, provides yet further evidence of the tensions and conflicts generated within local communities by the broader socio-economic pressures of the day. With the changes in the willingness of the Church to provide protective or counter-magic, the reforming clergy opposed the continuance of magical practices, together with the persistence of traditional forms of devotion that they held 'too many erroneous and foolish opinions'.

The majority of the people cited as witches during the Burning Times were ordinary people, and just how many of those hanged as such were genuine witches, we have no way of knowing. Genuine witches have always had a remarkable knack of 'going back into the shadows' when social pressures deem it necessary, and no doubt this inherent cunning that had kept them safe for hundreds of years, worked in their favour during the 'Burning Times'.

English witchcraft, however, had some distinctive features, and because of the national love of animals, every trial was replete with little domestic creatures cherished as household pets, referred to in the trials as imps, familiars or devils. One particularly damning piece of evidence against a witch was the existence of a toad as a close companion, which, in court records of the time, was identified as her familiar. Perhaps to the more sophisticated and worldly inquisitors the idea of keeping a toad as a pet was considered to be abnormal behaviour. To rural folk, however, the toad may have been performing its domestic duties since we know that these creatures were kept in larders and pantries to feed on flies and other insects. A recently redis-covered newspaper cutting records working toads being specially bred for the purpose of keeping greenhouses free of aphids after the First World War. The practice was widespread throughout the country 'particularly among the landed gentry with their steam-heated glass-houses'. Apparently toads could live to be 30 or 40 years old and were given names by the children with whom they became popular pets.

The Encyclopaedia of Witchcraft and Demonology also records that the art of pricking or discovering the 'Devil's mark' on the body of a witch, 'though practised on the Continent, was especially English; again, hardly a trial lacked this testimony'. Scratching a witch 'above breath' to negate her power, and forcing her to recite formulas that established her guilt were also peculiarly English. Or, as Robbins explains:

The relative simplicity of confessions and the absence of satanic rigmarole in English witch trials were due to the absence of a centralised, highly organised persecuting body, such as the Inquisition, which made all confessions conform to the pattern its demonologists had dreamed up ... the English Channel preserved England from the grosser manifestation of the delusion in the rest of Europe, and English witchcraft took on national characteristics ...

Research has shown that there were several peaks of persecution, with the greatest number of accusations of witchcraft in the reign of Elizabeth I; and rose again under Cromwell. The proportion of hangings to indictments shows that the most dangerous time to be a witch was the closing years of Elizabeth's reign; the first years of Charles I (41% were hanged) and the early Commonwealth. The greatest slaughter of witches came in the summer of 1645 ...

Even more terrible than fiction was the disturbing character of Matthew Hopkins, the Witch-Finder General, whose specialty was to round up those accused of witchcraft and subject them to the most humiliating public body-searches. In one year from 1645 to 1646 Hopkins 'sent to the gallows more witches than all the other witch-hunters of England'. Hundreds of women were dragged before a jeering mob and having had the clothes ripped from their backs, were made to undergo intimate searches for witch-marks. No doubt modern psychiatry would have a name for Hopkins' condition, but without fear of contradiction we may safely assume that his motivations were probably due more to sadistic leanings and greed than any great religious fervour.

The *stigmata diaboli,* or Devil's marks that were held up as evidence of witchcraft, ultimately led to the death of the accused. Warts, moles, old wounds, corns and birthmarks – common blemishes that adorn the bodies of *every human being in the world* – were considered marks of the Devil. Witchfinders were instructed to search in the most intimate places for such imprints, particularly the anus in men and the breasts and private parts of women. Not only were the accused stripped naked, every bit of hair was shaved from their bodies. The witches' mark was just as damning and any small protuberance on the body could be classed as a Devil's teat used for suckling familiars.

Pricking was the favourite method of uncovering witches and, in addition to Hopkins, there were plenty of other unpleasant characters about who set themselves up as roving 'finger men'. If the witch-hunter ran a pin into the flesh of an accused witch and the wound failed to bleed, this was taken as evidence of guilt.

There are in existence today, pricking instruments with retractable pins that were used to chalk up the numbers of guilty parties and earn the Witch-finders their gruesome fees.

There is a recorded instance where one of the hapless women found a champion in a certain Lieutenant Colonel Hobson who witnessed a respectable woman being subjected to 'pricking'. The lady in question ... 'in sight of all the people, he laid her body naked to the waist, with her clothes over her head, by which fright and shame, all her blood contracted into one part of her body.' The Witch-finder stabbing with his pin produced no sign of bleeding, but Hobson demanded that the woman be allowed to stand and that the pin be run into her thigh, which produced the required flow of blood to prove her innocence.

To correct a popular misconception, English witches were not burned alive at the stake – the universal practice elsewhere, including Scotland. Under English law, burning was the penalty for *petit-treason*; with supportive documentary evidence of women being found guilty of poisoning an unwanted spouse who suffered this penalty. Nor were there mass executions like those carried out in France and Germany. There were probably no more than a thousand people convicted and executed for witchcraft in England, but if we take away the pitiful minority who may possibly have committed murder, we are still left with a thousand innocent people dead as a result of religious bigotry.

By the time the throne passed to the House of Hanover in 1714, the witch-hunts had burned themselves out. The last person to be executed for witchcraft in England was Alice Molland in 1684, and the last indictment was against Jane Clerk in 1717 – but in this case, the lady got off. George II's Statute of 1736 repealed the archaic statute of 1604 but instead of abolishing the Witchcraft Act completely, it reversed it. No longer would the law punish witches, it would only turn its attention to those who thought they were witches! It was not until the world had seen two world wars and genocide of equal magnitude that the Witchcraft Act was finally repealed in 1951.

Summary

In an interview with Michael Howard for *The Cauldron,* Shani Oates, Maid of the Clan Tubal Cain, and successor of Evan John Jones, made a highly pertinent comment:

Traditional Craft has its roots in the post-witch-craze resurgence of the cunning folk traditions and folk magicks of the mid-1700s, a gritty and pragmatic craft at the popular level. Neo-paganism, conversely, was a middle-class, intellectual revival born of the Romantic Movement from around the same period. Wicca attempted to merge both paradigms in the mid-20th century, and all three have diverged yet further in principal if not in practice.

Michael Howard, however, reveals there is evidence for middle-class intellectuals involved in revivals of witchcraft in the 18th and 19th century before Wicca was ever created by Gardner. 'In fact I know of a traditional covine dating from the 19th century whose membership included local rustic types and middle-class occultists. A lot of Golden Dawn material was apparently introduced into the group at that time by one of their Magisters. This mixing of social classes is something I have noted as a pattern in my research into the Old Craft, and not all members of traditional covines were toothless yokels!'

From these comments, we can deduce that what most people now refer to as 'traditional witchcraft' dates from around this time. The building blocks of magical learning pouring in from all quarters was being assimilated into a coherent whole by interested parties – who may, or may not, have had any genuine witch-blood. Witchcraft *per se* was blooded but not bowed, and despite the horrors of the Burning Times, there were those who were willing to pick up the baton and continue the race – even though they ran under different rules.

In fairness to Margaret Murray's reporting, much of what she took to be claims of ancient lineage were the more recent spurious stories that had entered history, courtesy of the Inquisition, of what witches were *supposed* to do. When she was conducting her researches in the early part of the 1900s for *The Witch-Cult in Western Europe*, she was probably encountering the versions of witchcraft described above ... with a bit of embell-ishment thrown in for good measure.

But as Robin Briggs observes in *Witches & Neighbours*: 'Murray argued that witches were really worshippers of the ancient pagan cult of Diana and that the sabbat was a traditional fertility rite. Apart from the banal point that certain pagan tradi-tions had survived into Christian Europe, this is complete nonsense, based on systematic misrepresentation of the source material.' The problem we have here, of course, is that like the majority of academics who cut through the falsehood and fabri-cation, Briggs does not believe that witches actually exist!

The Story So Far ...

Nevertheless, genuine witches have always kept a low profile and, more often than not, the ancient beliefs they followed in secret ran alongside Christian beliefs, which they practised in public. One anonymous on-line contribution of an article from *Psychic News* revealed how a man had unconsciously absorbed the traditions of his valley through his father and paternal grand-parents. He was able to trace his family connections back to the 14th century but didn't realise just how firmly entrenched the traditions were until he left to travel the world.

You go away and become more sophisticated and educated and all the rest, but it is there and it very easily surfaces again. I don't disbelieve this stuff at all; it's there, it's part of your psyche. It's something you have got, and I don't think it is remotely connected with any of this modern neo-Celticism and New Age stuff. That just seems false. The stuff I have inherited was old, and it was the sort of thing which makes the hair on the back of your neck stand up. It still does with me ... There was a layer of belief when I was a kid that was not Christian, and that was old. People knew it wasn't Christian but they didn't regard it as being inimical to Christianity ... everybody that I knew were church or chapel-goers, but these were sort of two separate compartments in their lives. They kept to the old gods but won't even mention their names. It still goes on and it certainly did when I lived there. It was ... all to do with the *genius loci*, the spirits of the place ... and the other thing is that this sort of background survives whether you want it to or not, because you don't shake it off.

There will be those who empathise with these sentiments. Despite the centuries of persecution, the Old Ways and the 'Way of the Witch' (though no longer necessarily the same thing) have continued to survive in the remote valleys and mountainous regions because, as the man said: you can't shake it off if it's in the blood.

Michael Howard also observed that the above is 'fairly identical to some of the pronouncements made by the so-called 'Guardians' discovered by the late Dr Anne Ross in the 1970s. They were farming families living in the Peak District, Derbyshire who claimed to be Celtic survivalists and featured in a BBC television documentary in the *Chronicle* archaeological/history series. However they were very adamant they were not witches and what they did was not witchcraft! See David Clarke and Andy Roberts' book, *Twilight of the Celtic Gods: An Exploration of Britain's Hidden Pagan Traditions*, which contains very similar quotes from local people about surviving folk customs in the area.'

Similar to the Romany, who are acknowledged as having

certain powers but follow the religion of the locality in which they reside, these instances reveal that what outsiders would *consider* to be witchcraft are emphatically denied by the people who possess them. Witchcraft, as we know, is a *natural ability* and these small pockets have obviously preserved a certain amount of racial knowledge, minus the 'call of the Wyrd'. As the first quote commented: 'People knew it wasn't Christian but they didn't regard it as being inimical to Christianity ... everybody that I knew were church or chapel-goers, but these were sort of two separate compartments in their lives ...'

It reminds us how closely the Old Ways and the pre-Reformation Church had been in medieval times – and why many modern day Old Craft witches feel comfortable within the confines of an early Norman or Anglo-Saxon village church. It may even suggest the point at which the practice between the cunning-folk (who were ostensibly Christian) and witchcraft separated into two subtly different skeins.

Chapter Nine

An Idyll for the Misbegotten (Ritual Magic)

The Bible tells us how to go to Heaven, but not how the heavens go.
Galileo 1615 [quoting Cardinal Caesar Baronius]

During the 18th-19th centuries, England experienced an occult revival that included the re-establishment of three major esoteric traditions – Rosicrucianism, Freemasonry and Druidry. From ancient times intelligent men have struggled to reconcile the discoveries of science with religious belief, often paying with their lives when their revelations conflicted with Church doctrine. Despite this heretical pastime, in the age before Darwin many powerful clerics were also notable scientific scholars and leading scientists were often conventionally pious.

Confronted by the fact that our planet was older, more complicated, diverse and cruel than they had previously imagined, it was inevitable that questions about God and the Bible began to be more commonplace. According to *The Watch on the Heath*, by Keith Thomson, these learned men decided that science and religion *could* share a philosophical basis. They held that instead of denying God, a careful rational study of nature would confirm that life was the product of God's unique creation. This belief became known as natural theology.

And while *The Daily Telegraph's* obituary for Charles Darwin on 21st April 1882 states: 'That the doctrine of Evolution must prove in the main a true and enduring one is doubted to-day by few really competent minds ...', we must also remember that Darwin repeatedly stated his belief in a Creator, despite his agnostic leanings after publication of *On The Origin of the Species*. Despite the controversy that still rages fiercely over his theories, by the time Darwin died, the Church had pretty much accepted them. He was given a State funeral at Westminster Abbey: and opened the floodgates for other radical thinkers of the time.

The Rosicrucians, or the Fraternity of the Rosy Cross, are generally believed to be members of a German mystical or occult order that was re-activated during the second decade of the 17th century, but which could trace its origins back to the 15th century. According to the entry in *Man, Myth & Magic*, it is still widely believed that they possessed important and arcane wisdom that has been transmitted to their spiritual heirs and successors. It is from this Order that the belief in the existence of the 'Secret Chiefs' or 'Masters' entered into occult-lore via the machinations of Madame Blavatsky, founder of the Theosophical Society (1875). One of the most interesting features of the Christian Rosenkreuzer legend, however, is the persistence with which it has survived, particularly in circles identified with occultism.

There were, of course, many who wished to join the Rosicrucian brotherhood. Unable to identify a single person who belonged to it, let alone the slightest clue that would reveal where its 'headquarters' might be found, they printed pamphlets, mostly in the shape of letters, which, it was hoped, would eventually find their way to someone 'in authority'. Some of these announced that their respective writers were already members of the fraternity.
Ellic Howe, *Rosicrucians*

Since the early 1700s all manner of groups, fraternities and associations have incorporated the Rose Cross in their titles, but it wasn't until the 1770s that a German Masonic rite appeared that attracted the support of alchemists and occultists. There has also been an 'echo of something vaguely Rosicrucian' as a feature of Freemasonry's so-called High Degrees since the 1750s, and the Rose Croix degree, now the 18th in the Ancient and Accepted

Rite, made its first appearance in France c1754. According to Howe, however, the only fraternity that actually revived the legend in its rituals was the Hermetic Order of the Golden Dawn, the most renowned magical society of modern times. The Golden Dawn was magical not Masonic, but its founders were also enthusiastic Freemasons.

Freemasonry, of course, began in the Middle Ages as an early trade union and is neither a religion, nor a substitute for one. The tradition arose from wherever men were assembled for large-scale building works, such as a cathedral, and where masons required proof of professional skill before accepting an itinerant colleague as a master craftsman. If the newcomer knew the answers in their correct form to certain veiled questions, together with certain passwords and signs, it confirmed that he really was a Master Mason and master of his craft.

The first Grand Lodge was inaugurated in 1721 – the first Grand Master being the Duke of Montague and since then the office has always been held by one of noble or royal birth. Freemasonry spread to the continent and during the second half of the 18th century. Alongside the regular 'High Grade' Freemasonry there were, in both France and Germany, a number of Masonic sects that dabbled with alchemy and occultism. One particular strain is of interest: from as early as 1738, a rite of alchemical, occult and Egyptian references, with a structure of 90 degrees, was being developed by one Giuseppe Balsamo, better known as Cagliostro, a key occultist of his time. Very close to the Grand Master of the Order of the Knights of Malta, Cagliostro founded the Rite of High Egyptian Masonry in 1784. The merging of the rites of Memphis and Misraïm under the influence of General Garibaldi in 1881 formed the later Masonic Rite of Memphis-Misraim: and Egyptian symbolism was very important within the works of the Golden Dawn.

Founded in 1887, the Golden Dawn was a by-product of the Rosicrucian Society in England, having been established in 1866 by a group of Freemasons who were interested in occultism, spiritualism and esoteric symbolism. By the early 1880s it had progressed to the study of the Qabbalah, alchemical symbolism and traditional occultism. Although not a Masonic Lodge, membership was restricted to Freemasons, and its tri-part head included Dr William Westcott, a London Coroner, Samuel Liddell Mathers and Dr William Robert Woodman, an antiquarian scholar.

The founding of the Golden Dawn follows the mysterious pattern characteristic of the Rosicrucians after some cipher manuscripts were bought from a bookstall in Farringdon Street, London. An accompanying letter stated that whoever cared to decipher the text should communicate with a German who would provide further information. The deciphered text revealed five Masonic rituals that were later elaborated by Mathers and the poet W B Yeats, who also became a prominent member of the Order.

As well as Yeats and Mathers, other important writers also belonged to the Order – A E Waite, an esoteric author; the fantasy novelists Arthur Machen and Algernon Blackwood; and Aleister Crowley. The Rider-Waite tarot is the most popular deck in use in the English-speaking world, although more serious occultists may prefer Crowley's more spectacular, visionary Thoth tarot, which he referred to as *The Book of Thoth*, accompanied by a book of that title intended for use with the deck.

According to *The Occult Source Book*, the rituals themselves were not merely artificial or theatrical. 'They were intended to symbolise certain stages of enlightenment or mystical consciousness upon a certain cosmic pathway called the Tree of Life. The Tree of Life is, in itself, a key motif in the Qabalah, or Jewish mystery tradition, and represents ten levels of consciousness between man and Godhead.' Along with the Qabalah, the Order also studied alchemy and ceremonial magic, inspiring most of what is valuable in subsequent initiatory groups of the Western tradition. The predominating influence, however, was that of ancient Egypt and the first Golden Dawn Temple was that of Isis-Urania, which opened in London in 1888. Society of the time was obsessed with the 'Egyptian Revival' and it was appropriate that interest in the subject should have been revived at this time (*The Atum-Re Revival*).

Samuel Liddell MacGregor Mathers was the leading light of the Order – and also its destroyer. His university was the reading room at the British Museum, and he had a good working knowledge of French, Latin and Greek, Hebrew and Coptic. He translated *The Kabbalah Unveiled* (1887), not from the Hebrew *Zohar* but from Rosenroth's Latin version. Similarly, his translation of *The Book of the Sacred Magic of Abra-Melin the Mage* (1898) was taken from a French text in the Bibliothèque de l'Arsenal in Paris. The teaching and personality of Mathers influenced people of such diverse talents as W B Yeats, Aleister Crowley, Dion Fortune, Arthur Machen, Florence Farr, Annie E F Horniman, A E Waite and (briefly) H G Wells to name but a few. With his wife and priestess, Moina, he reintroduced the cult of Isis (although the rites were not Golden Dawn rituals) and originally performed them at their home in Paris.

The Egyptian Revival

Surprisingly, the Jesuits had shared certain interests with the Rosicrucians – with Hermetic and occult philosophies forming a considerable part of Jesuit missionary activity. In some instances Rosicrucian symbolism was also used by the Jesuits to show that the two Orders shared certain attributes, and further suggesting that the Rosicrucians were a power to be reckoned with. The philosophy, based on orthodox Roman Catholicism and the teaching of Hermes Trismegistus, claimed that the Egyptians were in the vanguard of metaphysical knowledge, and that it was to Egypt that we should look for the origins of art, science, and religion!

Research into the histories of Rosicrucianism and Freemasonry has been hindered by the enormous amounts of sensational, inaccurate media reporting, and so-called questionable 'occultist' publications. Nevertheless, the iconography of European Freemasonry was also steeped in Egyptian design, for Egypt provides the main source of Masonic doctrine, while Masonic tradition holds that Freemasonry is as old as the art and science of architecture, and so there is a debt to Egypt in perpetuality, as this author observes in *The Atum-Re Revival*.

The magic and mysticism of ancient Egypt was brought to the forefront of contemporary occultism in the 1800s. In Freemasonry and the Theosophist movement, the gods of Egypt re-emerged in ever-surprising guises, observed Erik Hornung in *The Secret Lore of Egypt: Its Impact on the West* – not to mention the impact on the magical teachings of the Golden Dawn and the writings of Aleister Crowley.

The interest in Egyptian ideas and objects often increased after some spectacular discovery – such as the *Mensa Isiaca* (or Bembine Tablet) or the Rosetta Stone.

Drawings, paintings and a developing appreciation of antiquity brought Egyptian motifs to a wider public throughout Europe. Nevertheless, from classical times, through the Renaissance, to the 18th century, to the revival period after the Napoleonic campaign, the 19th century continued with buildings, furniture, jewellery, etc., offering thousands of variations in the style; and with travel on the increase for the Victorians, strong Egyptian elements also crept into the paintings and literature of the time. 'By the 20th century, even cinemas and factories acquired the 'Nile style' veneer under the guise of Art Deco architecture,' explains Dr J C Curl in *The Egyptian Revival*.

The Egyptian influences continued to filter down through the embryonic organisations in the form of the syncretism of Fellowship of Isis and the Alexandrian traditions – and it is now common for magazine editors and publishers to be offered 'Egyptian Wicca' as an accredited belief system!

Western Ritual Magic

In ancient Egypt the system that we would now call 'ritual' or 'ceremonial' magic would have been an integral part of the inner Temple workings and the province of the higher priesthood. In the 1985 version of Christian Jacq's *Egyptian Magic,* Professor of Egyptology Rosalie David confirmed this opinion by writing in the introduction: 'In Egypt, magic was regarded as an exact science, in its highest form, its secrets were revealed only to the highest orders of the priesthood who thus had the ability to control and regulate events and actions.'

Right from the start, however, we should attempt to put this form of magic in its proper perspective because in modern occultism, the lines between belief and practice often become distorted. This is due to a basic lack of understanding of what constitutes natural ability, devotional observance and what can best be described as 'ritual magic'. Following the disintegration of the classical world, it might be true to say that in the separation of religion and magic, and the establishment of the early Church, the pursuit of ritual magic (in its ancient form) largely disappeared. Nevertheless, it continued among individuals and in small groups such as alchemists, the Templars, the Rosicrucians and later, the Freemasons, down through the centuries without any overtly religious overtones.

It was not until 19th century that the tradition that we identify as 'Western ritual magic' emerged; the latter half of the century seeing the inauguration of the Hermetic Order of the Golden Dawn, with its heavy overlay of Egyptian symbolism. Without a doubt, this Order, more than any other, has had a most profound effect on the development of ritual magic among the intellectuals of the time — and brought it, in its modern form, into the public eye. A number of other similar groups evolved to perpetuate the varying forms of Western ritual magic and although many of the schools that once flourished have now 'gone into the shadows', some continue to exist in hybrid form. The foremost among this group are the Freemasons who, although once a genuine school of ritual occultism, now shy away from acknowledging this aspect of their history, although a great deal of their symbolism still reflects the Egyptian influence.

What *Is* Ritual Magic?

Broadly speaking, ritual magic is an approach that employs the use of ritual, symbol and ceremony as a means of representing and communicating with forces underlying the universe and man — the macrocosm and the microcosm introduced by Robert Fludd. The ritual aspect is the process of dramatising the focus of what is being expressed so that the whole person (body, emotions and mind) is channelled into bringing about 'the total experience'. This type of ritual working draws on all the five senses, using all the methods of drama and all the techniques of religion — **without focusing on any particular religious belief**. The ritual magician directs his/her attention on symbols that are keys to the subconscious; they make it possible to communicate concepts and ideals *beyond* religious philosophy or intellectual understanding.

It is important to understand, however, that although a ritual magician is not required to follow a specific religion or devotional observance, they do believes in a 'Higher Power' on which to call during a ritual. But it is more than likely to be the deity that 'corresponds' with the *natural* energies of the cosmos, not a deity perceived for devotional purposes. This explains why much of what was originally made public concerning ritual magical practice was seen as satanic or Devil worship, since the magician was just as likely to call on a demon as an archangel.

But what exactly are these 'demons' of which we hear so much in connection with ritual magic? If we examine the characteristics of those in Aleister Crowley's *Goetia*, each one represents the exaggerated aspects of the things most people strive for under normal circumstances: knowledge, wealth, ambition, a loving partner, etc. If these desires become distorted to the point of obsession, the thirst for them becomes a corruptive and insatiable desire for magical understanding, fabulous wealth, unlimited power and licentious sex.

The 'evil' spirits or demons of *Goetia* are thereby recognised as portions of the human brain; the correspondences are methods of stimulating or regulating these particular areas. Using the example given for invoking Cimieries gives a better understanding of the demon itself. Cimieries is the 'spirit force' governing logic, grammar and rhetoric and therefore refers to the portion of the brain that 'sub-serves the logical facility'. The Invocation of Cimieries can reasonably be used to stimulate and develop these attributes in an individual to enhance his or her career; *over*-stimulation, however, could result in megalomania especially as he is depicted as a valiant warrior riding on a black horse.

In many cases, the misrepresentation has grown from academic interpretations of old *grimoires* and histories taken from the likes of John Dee, Paracelsus, Eliphas Levi and Crowley, but written by those with no formal magical training. Magic, and especially ritual magic, by its very nature is obtuse – it is also the last great adventure – so what hope do non-initiates have in understanding the cosmic mysteries that the adept strives to explore?

For example, Professor Elizabeth Butler might have been a Faust scholar, but it was scant qualification for her to write on the subject of *Ritual Magic* with any real degree of **Understanding**. From the historical perspective, however, she is worthy of note as her introductory observations show: 'That so-called 'black' magic is rarely as black as it has been painted is one of the conclusions to which I have been irresistibly drawn by a close scrutiny of the texts available; but folly is on the whole more prevalent than vice, as the 'black' rituals abundantly prove.' Nevertheless, this did not prevent her from stating that Crowley 'did his ineffective best to set the myth of Satanism in circulation again in a positive spate of pagan, Gnostic, pantheistic, Qabalistic and generally speaking synthetic ritual processes' to demonstrate that she had learned little about *practical working* magic from her research – or anything about Aleister Crowley either!

The Druidic Revival

Legend has it that Druidry had survived the massacre of the druidic priesthood on Anglesey by the Roman legions, and that the Mysteries of Ceridwen were still being practised in Snowdonia as late as the 13th century. Allegedly, Welsh druids had founded the Mount Haemus Grove in Oxford around the same time; and that prominent Rosicrucian, Freemason, astrologer and founder of the Royal Society, Elias Ashmole, was a member of the Grove in the 17th century. The 18th century revival was spearheaded by intellectual luminaries such as the Reverend William Stukeley, who was also a Freemason and founder of the Society of Antiquaries, and the visionary poet and artist William Blake, both of whom were 'Chosen Chiefs' of the Ancient Druidic Order (ADA)

Another leading light was Edward Williams, better known as Iolo Morganwg, who claimed to have been taught about the Bardic tradition by several native Welsh poets who had inherited the knowledge from original sources. One of these bards is purported to have given Iolo a cache of documents describing the procedures of ancient druidic ceremonies that had kept the tradition of the Eisteddfodau alive from Celtic times, through the Middle Ages and up to the 18th century.

Critics have pointed out that Iolo Morganwg's Ancient British Bardic Order (ABBO) was also modelled on the structure of Freemasonry. It has three grades or degrees – bard, ovate and druid – which his detractors say had never existed in ancient druidism, and had been copied from the Masonic degrees of entered apprentice, journeyman and master mason. Welsh scholars subsequently claimed that he was a master forger and faked many of the manuscripts he claimed to have found. Nevertheless, from these highly suspect beginnings, the modern Gorsedd of Bards has grown, with a membership drawn from the intellectual and cultural elite of Wales, including the former Archbishop of Canterbury, Dr Rowan Williams.

The most dramatic occasion in the ADA was the decision to appoint the controversial George Watson (McGregor) Reid as its Chosen Chief in 1909. Reid took the ADA out of the shadows by making the decision that the Order would celebrate the Summer Solstice at Stonehenge, which they did from 1909 onwards. Reid took the name 'McGregor' because of his own Scottish roots, and his friendship with Samuel McGregor Mathers of the Hermetic Order of the Golden Dawn, and also introduced a triple system based on the grading of Golden Dawn.

During Reid's and his son Robert's stint as Chosen Chiefs, the Order included many of the well-known names in occultism but politics intervened and in 1964, following the death of Robert Reid, the different factions went their separate ways. Ross Nichols formed the Order of Bards, Ovates and Druids (OBOD) using the three grades introduced by Iolo Morganwg; observing seasonal rites with a new set of rituals that were said to have been written by the celebrated ceremonial magician, Madeline Montalban. It has also been claimed that these contemporary rituals also influenced the creation of Gerald Gardner's neo-pagan Wicca.

As with their Elizabethan counterparts, the study of mysticism and magic remained the province of the learned men of the time, since only the privileged had the education that enabled them to translate the rare Greek, Latin or Hebrew manuscripts, or travel to far-off places to observe the wonders of

Eastern esoteric traditions.

Summary

Karl Marx described religion as 'the opium of the people'. Opium is a hallucinatory drug that gives a feeling of well-being; it produces illusions which distort reality. Marx believed that religion gives a false picture of society and prevents people from seeing the truth, providing an illusion of happiness and an imaginary escape from problems. So many elements of the Rosicrucian, Freemasonry, Theosophy and Druidry crept into the magical orders and revivalist witchcraft that the 'new beliefs' disappeared behind their own curtain of illusion. Occultism was the new opiate of the thinking classes.

It was easy for the founders to bamboozle eager new members who applied to join the various Orders, since by manipulating the rites of Freemasonry, they could present a complete set of principles as received wisdom. They could trawl the libraries for obscure classic manuscripts to provide new rites and incorporate elements of Eastern esoteric practice to add to the mystery and pass it all off as being part of an authentic ancient tradition. Many of these components can still be found in contemporary Wicca, despite the effort made by Doreen Valiente to weed out Gardner's original rites – especially the input from Aleister Crowley!

Around 1886, however, Charles G Leland had made the acquaintance of an Italian *strega* (witch) by the name of Maddalena, whom he employed to collect 'spells in many places all the traditions of the olden times known to them'. After many years (1897), his contact sent him what is now known as *Aradia: the Gospel of the Witches*, although Leland was convinced by the genuineness of the information, he revealed a certain scepticism in his preface as to the manuscript's authenticity.

Nevertheless, the text reveals that Diana is the goddess of the Old Religion, with Aradia, her daughter; that one of the ceremonies is the 'conjuration of Cain'; and the 'benediction of the honey, meal and salt, or the Cakes of the Witch supper' – all echoes found in contemporary witchcraft. According to Leland: 'The Gospel of the Witches, as I have given it, is in reality only the initial chapter of the collection ... the whole of which are in the main to be found in my *Etruscan Roman Remains* and *Florentine Legends* ...'

The Story So Far ...

As we discussed at the beginning of *Traditional Witchcraft and the Witchcraft Revival*, the introduction of a contemporary eclectic, pick-and-mix approach that maintains that all universal god/desses are one, and that any permutation will do when it comes to supplication, is a long way from the truth. At the advanced academic, theological, or higher ritual magic end of the spectrum this may be the case but at grass roots level, where most of us operate, it is essential to understand which deity (or force) represents a particular psychic energy.

It is also necessary to repeat the extract from *Coven of the Scales: The Collected Writings of A R Clay-Egerton*, because the Clay-Egertons did not advocate what is now referred to as 'eclectic paganism'. What they *did* teach was the desire for knowledge and experience, regardless of source. Each new experience was studied *within* the confines of that particular religion, path or tradition. **Each discipline was kept completely separate from another.** It was only when a student had a *thorough* understanding of the tenets of each discipline were they encouraged to formulate them into their own individual system.

As a result, their own system of Old Craft teaching was a direct link to the 'Cheshire coven' that the under-age Bob Clay-Egerton was initiated into in 1941, and which itself could be traced back to the early-mid 1880s from the location of Alderley Edge. The Cheshire coven had received an influx of members in the late 1880s when Welsh miners were brought in from the historic Parys Mountain copper mines in Anglesey. He quickly became aware that some of the witches were members of a separate magical order and was initiated into that in the summer of 1943.

The Alderley Edge deposits have been mined since the Bronze Age, and coupled with 'a curious tradition which preserves a very ancient fragment of mythological belief' – the legend of the Wizard of Alderley Edge – and the series of tragic accidents (which gained the mines a notoriety that continues to haunt them), led to the West and Wood mines being finally blocked in the early 1960s. The Clay-Egertons re-emerged in the 1960s in Warwickshire, and it was from there that the Moonraker coven was 'driven out of town' by anti-occult hysteria, and the couple moved to Newcastle-upon-Tyne. Needless to say, Bob Clay-Egerton, who died in 1998, witnessed at lot of changes since he became a witch in pre-Gardnerian times. He wrote:

Beliefs change and so do practices. There must be constant change and growth for progression, or decay sets in – although some changes do not flourish and die out. Others flourish, but change gradually, some out of all recognition. From my knowledge of my own Cheshire coven, and those I visited in Shropshire and North Wales, plus what I have ascertained from subsequent contact with people in their late 70s, 80s and 90s who claim membership of the Old Craft, there were differences in practice between covens. Northern covens seem to have called their groups *cuveens*, or *courveens* – so practices in the South of England may well have differed considerably from those in the Midlands and North.

In an article published in *The Bridge* (1994) he observed that what he knew of contemporary Old Craft came from three sources. His own experience dating from 1941; what he had been told of coven history; and what he had learned from Old Crafters who had contacted him over the years in response to his writings in occult magazines. Nevertheless, there are numerous echoes of *Aradia* in British Old Craft. For example:

- Leland's Notes to Chapter 13, which includes: 'If thou are favourable and wilt grant my prayer. Then may I hear/The bark of a dog/The neigh of a horse/The croaking of a frog/The chirp of a bird ...', which is still extant in Old Craft Circles at the conclusion of a magical working. [This author knew from a child that if you offered up a 'prayer' outside in the fields or woods, the bark of a dog/fox, the cry of an owl/buzzard, or croak of a frog/toad, was the sign your 'prayer' had been heard – MD]

- Leland also reveals: 'The most important part of witchcraft is to intone or accent the incantations accurately, in a manner like that of Church chanting or Arab recitations ...' hence the rhythmic form of most spells.

- Another observation that is also pertinent to Old Craft is the *commanding* of a deity to grant a spell or request, 'The magus or witch, worships the spirit, but claims to have the right, drawn from a higher power, to compel even the Queen of Earth, Heaven and Hell to grant the request ...' as being strictly according to ancient magical techniques as described by classic authorities.

- There is even an oblique reference to the Mysteries of witchcraft in relation to the symbolic conjuration of the bread being 'deeply sacred because it [the grain] had lain in the earth, where dark and wondrous secrets bide ... It is a type of resurrection from the earth, and was therefore used at the Mysteries ... and the grain to chthonic secrets, or to what had been under the earth in darkness ... a kind of wild poetry based on symbols, all blending into one another, light and darkness, fire-flies and grain, life and death ...'

- What is known today as a hag-stone was referred to by Leland as a 'Holy-stone' and to find a stone with a hole in it was a special sign of favour.

On a final point, the majority of prayers, spells, and invocations used in modern-day witchcraft are relatively recent compilations since nothing pertaining to Old Craft was ever written down. Books on Wicca are keen to mention the *Book of Shadows*, but as Bob Clay-Egerton wrote in *What You Call Time*: 'I do not know of the keeping of any distinct *Book of Shadows*. True, some witches in some covens did keep notes of recipes for cooking, or for medications, but I know of no record being kept of rituals, at least in Old Craft.'

Chapter Ten

Dream Sequence (Modern)

... In the deep, dank recesses of the imagination there is always the vision of a vaulted subterranean chamber. The impenetrable stone walls suppurating moisture like globules of blood, glisten in the candle-light, as flickering cowled shadows perform a sinister dance macabre by the high altar. The fetid air mingles with the reek of incense as the high priest prepares to conduct the most blasphemous of all satanic rites of the Witches' sabbat – the Black Mass ...
Udolpho [Journal of the Gothic Society]

It was only through the medium of low-cost printing that the Victorians were able to record a great deal of information concerning such subjects as fortune-telling and folklore for posterity. Public taste for the esoteric had undergone a large-scale renaissance: folklore and mythology was back in fashion; spiritualism was the new rock-n-roll; Fraser's *Golden Bough* was a best-seller and Conan Doyle was seeing fairies at the bottom of the garden. Unfortunately, Victorian sensibility ensured that most of what appeared in printed form was so pasteurised, homogenised and tied up in Christian red tape, that from the genuine seeker's point of view, it was next to useless – and much of what appears in contemporary pagan publishing is still firmly rooted in those Victorian sources.

Astrological correspondences played an important part in ritual magic and, although the practice was an ancient art, by the time of the Renaissance it was treated with contempt. It wasn't until 1951 when the Witchcraft Act was repealed in Britain, that casting horoscopes professionally became legal and gained a certain kudos when C G Jung referred to it as a *scientia intuitiva* – an intuitive science which he used to point out elements in his patients' personalities that might be of use in psychoanalysis.

As far as Craft was concerned, it's probably fair to say that the general public were first made aware of contemporary witchcraft when Gerald Gardner, a retired civil servant, published *Witchcraft Today* in 1954. He related how he had been initiated into a New Forest coven and in 1959 published a second book, *The Meaning of Witchcraft*, in which he reiterated his statements about 'the healthy, natural religion of Wicca', and set out to show that Wicca had been established from early pre-Christian times ... worshipping the Horned God and the Mother Goddess.

Gardner's claims were quickly endorsed by Dr Margaret Murray, a highly respected anthropologist who, in several books expounded on the idea that witchcraft was a survival of the pagan religion of Europe. Although Murray's theory was not accepted by fellow academics, most budding witches of the time clung firmly to her writings as an endorsement for their claims.

By the time of his death in 1964, the Gardnerian Tradition was represented in most parts of Britain and he left his Witchcraft Museum at Castletown, on the Isle of Man, to his High Priestess, Monique Wilson. In 1970, *Frontiers of Belief* editor, Frank Smyth, observed wryly: 'Various other followers benefited through [Gardner's] Will ... seemed to indicate that witchcraft was a paying proposition and many of his followers made haste to jump on the bandwagon, appearing on television, writing articles in the Press, and in some cases bringing out their own books on the subject.'

Frontiers of Belief makes interesting reading. It was released as a companion volume to the unique esoteric encyclopaedia *Man, Myth & Magic* and reflected the general perception of occult matters of the time ... but re-reading it reveals that very little has changed *since* the 1970s. 'Most British witches, despite their constant assertions that they are 'hereditary' followers of their craft, are former members of one orthodox Church or another ... [while] schism in one form or another has split the witchcraft

movement several times since Gardner first published his beliefs
...'

To the many who accept Gardner's theories, he is considered a 'brilliant scholar and a much maligned individual' but in *Man, Myth & Magic* Frank Smyth suggests that in the absence of any concrete evidence, there is a strong case for believing that Gardner invented the modernised cult of Wicca to satisfy his own sense of the esoteric. His rituals were far more heavily based on sex than others practised at the time, and Smyth concludes that it is reasonable to suppose that Gardner's sexual whims were gratified by the religion he had created. Francis King in *Ritual Magic in England* pulled no punches in accusing him of being: 'A sado-masochist with both a taste for flagellation and marked voyeuristic tendencies.'

Common to all, however, was the introduction of elaborate ceremony and ornate regalia, with High Priestesses clad in luxurious robes (or appearing naked in the more sensationalist magazines and supplements) 'sporting red garters around their naked thighs and multi-coloured girdles around their midriffs. Silver or amber necklaces dangle between their breasts, and in their right hands they hold the magic Athame, or ritual knife. The High Priests are crowned with horned helmets and armed with double-edged swords, and the coven's dancing, naked and chanting, around altars littered with incense thuribles, chalices, pentacles and magical bowls of salt and water.' Added to this, some groups leaned more towards ritual magic, astrology and other occult practices to a much greater degree than the original Gardnerian movement. Michael Howard, prolific author, editor of *The Cauldron* since 1976 and a Gardnerian witch since 1969, puts the roots of the tradition into perspective:

It can be claimed that Gerald Gardner joined a 'traditional' coven in the New Forest in 1939, whose membership was made up of local rural witches and incoming theosophical occultists. It is unproven whether the group was descended from one of the Nine Covens allegedly founded by the Essex cunning man Old George Pickingill (as has been claimed since the 1970s by E W Liddell) but the latest research by Philip Heselton seems to suggest that some members of New Forest did follow a pre-existing family tradition. Several well-known Wiccans such as Patricia Crowther, Lois Bourne, Eleanor Bone and Doreen Valiente have also claimed contact with pre-Gardnerian witches. Crowther with a hereditary witch called Jean McDonald in Scotland; Bone with a war-time group in Cumbria; Bourne with Monica English's old Grey Goosefeather coven in Norfolk; and Valiente with Robert Cochrane's Clan of Tubal Cain.

In later years, the Gardnerian Tradition was eclipsed by the Alexandrian cult, led by Manchester born Alex Sanders and his wife, Maxine. The Alexandrians continued the Gardnerian practice of working naked, or 'sky-clad', and were far more geared to cope with the attendant publicity that their leader courted. In fairness, no one considered the late Alex Sanders powers as affectation – it was his overt dedication to tasteless showmanship that non-Alexandrians found offensive. In an open letter (1991) to several pagan magazines, Patricia Crowther reminded readers that Sanders had been responsible for some of the most adverse publicity ever aimed at the Craft during the 1960s and did more to harm embryonic paganism than anything its enemies could have invented. A flair for showmanship meant that Alex Sanders was never out of the media spotlight and appeared on many of the influential programmes of the time. Jimmy Savile featured him in a controversial radio interview; he was a guest on the popular Simon Dee television show and perhaps the most surprising of all, an appearance on Joan Bakewell's BBC *Late Night Line-Up*.

With the publication of two books featuring the couple *(King of the Witches* by June Johns and *Maxine, the Witch Queen)* the popular concept of sexual activity playing an important role in witchcraft was as strong as ever. To those outside Craft, modern Wicca, under its trappings of a rejuvenated ancient fertility cult, was merely an excuse for sexual excess. Although, as Robert Cochrane remarked, there had been no cause for a fertility religion in Europe since the advent of the coultershare plough in the 13th century, the public and, of course, the Church, still preferred to see witchcraft as being inextricably bound up with unbridled sex and Devil-worship.

In stark contrast, in his book *Witchcraft: A Tradition Renewed*, Evan John Jones describes the natural worship of the Triple Goddess (as maiden, mother and crone – symbolised by the waxing and waning of the moon) and her consort the Horned God (in his dual aspects as the Green Man and the Dark Lord of the Wild Hunt – representing the deity of fertility and death). However, to refer to the witchcraft revival as merely a throwback to an ancient fertility cult totally avoids the mystical importance surrounding the belief, for this was *never* a simple rustic faith of peasants. The faithful still revered all aspects of nature, whether beautiful, bountiful or bloodstained; following the cycles of the seasons in the observation of birth, death and rebirth as represented by the turning of the year.

According to Jones, of equal importance was the recognition of the darker, more mystical side of life, receptive to hidden psychic forces and 'the ability to understand that, behind the veil between the known and the unknown worlds of the natural and supernatural, there are powers which were once the birthright of humanity ...' It was this dark side that also required the sacrifice of the Divine King in order that his followers might survive having eaten of his flesh; and the God-King sacrificing his own life so that his people may live is a recurring theme among ancient civilisations.

This mystical or Mystery aspect of paganism appears to be

one that is assiduously avoided by all but a few of the more traditionally minded. The late Robert Cochrane was highly critical of the development of the modern Craft in an article written as early as 1964 for *Pentagram* ('The Craft Today'); describing it as an attempt by 20th century man to deny the responsibilities of the 20th century. He felt that many witches had turned their backs on the reality of the outside world, pursuing a belief system that failed to recognise the needs of modern living, whilst repeating rituals by rote, rather than by understanding. In consequence, he believed that much of it had become 'static and remote from its original purpose, which was to enlighten the follower spiritually'.

Evan John Jones, who was a member of Cochrane's coven, contends that behind the simplicity of it all was a deeper faith that called for a greater understanding than blind acceptance, which ably demonstrates that dedicated pagans are not expected to accept 'the word' in its fundamental context. Beneath the exterior of a simple nature worship and cosy sabbat ceremonies, there lies a deeper tradition through which the devotee 'may perceive the beginnings of that ultimate in wisdom, knowledge of themselves and of their motives'.

In a further article for *Pentagram* ('The Faith of the Wise') Cochrane attacked the limited perception of the various 'authorities' on witchcraft, since being one of the oldest and most 'potent' of religions, it was a way of life 'different and distinct from any theory promulgated by the authorities or historians ...' According to Cochrane it brought 'Man into contact with Gods, and Man into contact with Self.. It creates within the human spirit a light that brightens all darkness, and which can never again be extinguished. It is never fully forgotten and never fully remembered.'

It was generally felt that, although controversial, outspoken, and virtually unknown outside traditional Craft, Cochrane could have been an important influence on breaching the divide between the different factions – despite his sarcastic comments about modern Wicca, which caused considerable offence amongst the Gardnerians of the time. Unfortunately, he died in 1966, and shortly after his death two ex-members of his coven, Ronald 'Chalky' White and George Stannard joined with Gerard Noel and Madge Worthington and founded The Regency. They claim that its 'inner circle was a direct continuation of Cochrane's Royal Windsor Cuveen' (*Genuine Witchcraft Explained*, John of Monmouth).

Of Cochrane, Doreen Valiente wrote: 'There is one thing I know for certain, Robert Cochrane 'had something'. Call it magical power, charisma or what you will. He may have been devious; but he was no charlatan.' More and more of his collected teachings on his beliefs and workings are now available to serious researchers, and it is Cochrane's flesh and blood interpretation of traditional Craft doctrine that inspires more credibility than the milk and water variety offered by many other pagan viewpoints.

Contemporary witchcraft, however, has not been without its persecutions and much of the ill-feeling between 'the old brigade' and the new, depends on which side of the great pagan divide individual witches found themselves. An anti-occult campaign had erupted during the 1960s and although Craft members sustained their fair share of casualties, it was nothing compared with the all-out, frontal assault that took place between 1988 and 1993. Hysteria-mongering evangelical Christians had prepared their infamous dossier with the help of several quisling occultists, who had provided a valuable insight into the pagan scene. In reality, this dossier was simply a potted review of pagan organisations, businesses, publications and individuals, but it was used by anti-occult campaigners as 'evidence' of the upsurge in witchcraft – which they considered to be the same as satanism.

The use of the printed word to inflame the populace against witchcraft is not a new idea. By the time Caxton's printing press had revolutionised people's access to reading matter, there were those ready to use the new contraption for more ominous purposes. Graphic pamphlets containing the confessions of witches helped to promote witch-hysteria across the country, culminating in localised support for the Witch-finders. And, as with the present day's sensational journalism which inflamed the anti-occult campaign out of all proportion, blame can be laid squarely at the doors of the authors of those early pamphlets who were responsible for inciting normal, average citizens to commit acts of persecution against their neighbours.

Understandably these new allegations gained a great deal of coverage in the press (both intellectual and tabloid) and much television and radio exposure. Then suddenly it was over ... and all that was left was a deafening silence. Accusations evaporated, accusers were mute and society carried on as though nothing had happened. From the very beginning the one thing that was apparent to anyone with any *real knowledge* of Craft, was the lack of factual, inside information concerning the practice of contemporary witchcraft. The experts so freely quoted by the media knew as much about the subject as Genghis Khan knew about community work, and the majority of those publicity-seeking individuals who gave interviews about their pagan beliefs did nothing to convince the public that the pagan world was not populated by lunatics.

In an open letter to *The Lamp of Thoth* magazine many years ago, Michael Howard commented:

Personally I have no wish to be associated with the many self-appointed spokespersons who claim to represent the Old Ways in the public eye ... Since I first became involved in the pagan movement in the early 1960s, there have been numerous attempts to unify pagans or promote a better image. These have failed for a variety of reasons, not the least because paganism (like the occult *per se)* attracts more than its fair share of cranks ...We are not supposed to say this but if you have been around a long time you will recognise it as a fact. Because of the high profile of this type of person, they tend to attract media coverage because basically they make a good story. That is all the average media hack is ultimately after. Journalists do not give a shit about the spiritual aspects of the Old Ways and – to be 100% honest – neither do many (not all, of course) of the witches and pagans they interview.

And in a personal letter written shortly before his death, Evan John Jones made a similar observation: 'Frankly, I don't think that things have changed all that much since the 60s, people are still bickering and back-biting as much as they did then. The only things that seems to have changed are the names of the people concerned.'

If we return to the points made by David V. Barrett in Chapter One (*The New Believers*), then we must accept that vast majority of present-day esoteric and pagan movements are eclectic. They do borrow from different traditions and from movements only slightly earlier than themselves. This goes a long way to explain why schisms and offshoots are frequent; partly, Barrett suggests, 'because of the unorthodox nature of both the beliefs and the believers'.

Summary

Contemporary witchcraft and Wicca have always been hard pressed to offer followers some form of coherent belief system and because of the lack of genuine traditional material, it meant that the followers could use whatever they felt conveyed the emotional or mystical need of the moment – a favourite piece of poetry or prose; invocations from the numerous books on witchcraft or magic; self-composed chants specifically written for the purpose. Then someone discovered Robert Graves' *The White Goddess* ... and the robbing of Graves began.

In a letter to Alan Richardson, dated 1989, Bill Gray wrote: 'Incidentally, I've solved the question why Roy Bowers [Robert Cochrane] chose the name Tubal Cain. He simply picked it out of *The White Goddess* as a smith-god because it happened to be there. Had it been Vulcan or Hephaestus, it might have been them instead.'

Michael Howard added: 'Bill Gray may be right that Cochrane took the name Tubal Cain from Graves (although there is no evidence to support that statement), but if he did *why* he picked it is more important and relevant. As a young man he worked as a blacksmith for London Transport and that experience may have influenced him. Also the symbolism of the lame smith-god exists in Traditional Craft – probably derived from Freemasonry and also the Society of the Horseman's Word, which Cochrane claimed to have family connections to.'

Despite Gray's observation, however, *The White Goddess* (originally published in 1948), became one of the most influential books on emerging paganism during the 1960 and 1970s. Robert Graves described *The White Goddess* as 'a historical grammar of the language of poetic myth', drawing from the mythology and poetry of Wales and Ireland, as well as that of Western Europe and the ancient Middle East. It is an essay upon the nature of poetic myth-making and based on earlier published articles; revised, amended and enlarged in 1966, it represented an approach to the study of mythology from the author's decidedly 'creative and idiosyncratic perspective'.

It suggests the existence of a European deity – a 'White Goddess of Birth, Love and Death', inspired and represented by the phases of the moon, and who, Graves argued, lies behind the faces of the diverse goddesses of various European mythologies. The original working title was *The Roebuck in the Thicket*; renamed *The Three-Fold Muse*, and finally *The White Goddess*, before being sent to the publishers. Although Graves' theories were rooted in a deep knowledge of ancient cultures of Greece and Rome, and some of his ideas have since been discredited by academics working in these fields, *The White Goddess* remains a fascinating account of the roots of poetic inspiration.

As Graves admitted, he was not a medieval historian, but a poet, and based his work on the premise that the language of poetic myth in the Mediterranean and Northern Europe was a magical language bound up with popular religious observations in honour of the moon-goddess, or Muse, some of them dating from the Old Stone Age, and that this remains the language of true poetry ... He went on to argue that 'true' or 'pure' poetry is inextricably linked with the ancient cult-ritual of his 'White Goddess and her son', and his conclusions come from his *own conjectures* about how early religions developed, as there is no historical evidence that a 'White Goddess' as he describes her, ever figured in any actual belief system.

Nevertheless, countless 'traditions', especially those reflecting goddess-spirituality, have robbed Graves relentlessly, despite the fact that he is alleged to have been unhappy with the published result. Some years later, however, the success of the book obviously changed his mind and he was discussing the concept of the White Goddess 'alter ego', the Black Goddess of Wisdom and the possibility of devoting one of his Oxford lectures to her. As Peter Kane observes (*The Cauldron*, No 133 2009): 'It is interesting that a book that was first conceived as a history of the origins and development of poetry should have ended up having such an important influence on one of the most intriguing forms of alternative spirituality to have emerged in the 20th century.' In over 60 years since its first publication the book has gone through four editions, in 1948, 1952, 1960 and 1997, and is still in print for future generations of pagans to plunder.

In stark contrast to the growing popularity of Wicca, by the turn of the 20th century the number of cunning folk across Britain had diminished drastically and by the 1940s they had 'essentially vanished from the country'. Owen Davies believed that the 'primary reason was the declining belief in the existence of malevolent witchcraft in the country (something brought about by modernisation and increasing education and literacy rates), and therefore the collapse of any need for anti-witchcraft measures that the cunning folk offered as their primary service'.

Although many of their magical practices were being absorbed into the growing number of 'alternative movements' of neo-paganism such as Wicca, another reason for the decline might be the fact that the basic belief of the cunning folk was Christianity, which 20th century neo-paganism was rejecting wholesale. As Ronald Hutton suggests, 'the cunning craft, rather than dying out, 'changed character' by being absorbed into other magical currents'.

The Story So Far ...

As many of contemporary pagan factions lack the 'power' of genuine traditional witchcraft, a large number of people are gravitating towards any advertisement in the pagan press that hints of 'Old Craft' and it soon becomes apparent that they are drawn to what they see as a 'power trip' rather than any dedication to preserving the Old Ways. Needless to say, it is when the pushing and badgering fails to gain admittance that they walk away in a huff to broadcast the message that there was 'nothing to be learned there, anyway'. And this is as it should be.

As we discussed at the beginning, there are different strands of approach in modern paganism:

- **Animistic:** The belief that everything animate and inanimate has its own lifeforce, such as that which forms the basis of shamanism and Old Craft;
- **Eclectic:** Selecting or borrowing from a variety of styles, systems, theories, beliefs, etc., as commonly found in modern paganism and Wicca;
- **Syncretic:** The attempt to reconcile different systems of

belief; the fusion or blending of religions, as by identification of gods, taking over of observances, or selection of whatever seems best in each; often producing a seemingly illogical compromise in belief. Found in many aspects of Western Ritual Magic, and the initiatory branches of traditional witchcraft;

- **Synergetic**: Combined or co-ordinated action; increased effect of two elements obtained by using them together. The combining of ancient wisdom with modern magical applications, as in the case of the contemporary approaches of Old Craft, Norse (Heathen) and Druidry.

Further evidence of these differences manifest in unexpected corners. For example: when writing the 'Traditional Witchcraft' series one of the editors suggested that a disclaimer be included when giving instructions for the use of feathers in a spell, because it might involve a 'Health and Safety' issue! A similar observation was made in relation to a text on 'cursing' whereby it was suggested that academic references should be included to show that these were historical sources! For the record, *no* self-respecting Old Craft witch is going to worry about government officialdom, or from throwing a curse if the occasion warrants it.

These are 'old' traditions and the roots go deep …

- Charles G Leland made another very pertinent observation in his Appendix to *Aradia*: 'What is remarkable, even to the being difficult to understand, is the fact that so much antique tradition survived with so little change among the peasantry. But legends and spells in families of hereditary witches are far more likely to live than fashions in art, yet even the latter have been kept since 2,000 years.'
- Animism, the ancient path of the shaman, is the belief that every object, animate and inanimate, has its own life-force, or energy. Here there is no separation between the spiritual

or physical world, where 'spirit' exists in all flora and fauna (including humans), rocks, geological features such as mountains, rivers and springs; and in natural phenomena such as storms, wind and the movement of heavenly bodies. It is the understanding that a small quartz pebble can link us with the cosmic Divine remains extant within modern Old Craft.

These were the lessons taught by Bob and Mériém Clay-Egerton. That it wasn't necessary to rely on ritual, circle casting, chanting and dancing to generate magical energy, it is there, all around us on a permanent basis. It means that a natural witch can be on her contacts in seconds; knowing what type of energy is needed to cure a headache, or channel the strength to walk the death-path with confidence after being diagnosed with a terminal illness. **It really is a belief that can move mountains – if the application is right.** These seemingly insurmountable obstacles do not necessarily mean that the doors to Old Craft are permanently barred. For those with the 'taint' of faere blood, the road may be long and arduous but the true seeker will get there in the end – and will not regret the struggles and hardship.

Chapter Eleven

Zeitgeist (Epilogue)

Within the span of human time, recorded 'fact' can be suspect.
So much is 'known' that isn't there. So much erased as 'incorrect'.
Dr Harold Selcon, *The Physicians of Myddfai*.

As I observed at the beginning ... it would be a grave error of judgement for anyone to claim that any branch of traditional witchcraft can trace its origins back to the Stone Age. In fact as the religious correspondent for *The Daily Telegraph* observed when reviewing the *Very Short Introduction to Paganism*, it would be scarcely more than a pamphlet if it were confined to paganism lived as a religion in the modern world, since Wicca, the modern form, goes back as far as 1948. 'In that year Gerald Gardner ... devoted himself to the witchcraft he claimed was the old religion of Europe.'

Professor Owen Davies, the author of this *Very Short Introduction to Paganism* says that no matter the depth of Gardner's deception and invention in creating Wicca, 'he spawned the development of a vibrant new pagan religion that would, over the next few decades, generate numerous variants and pathways under the umbrella of 'witchcraft'.' One might mention the internet's role in propagating Wiccan notions of religious history, claims Davies, also noting that television programmes such as *Buffy, the Vampire Slayer* and *Sabrina the Teenage Witch* 'normalised the idea of Wiccan magic for tens of millions of viewers, though without really portraying Wicca as a pagan *religion* as distinct from a mere source of spells'.

One of these 'variants' is the Fellowship of Isis, inaugurated at Clonegal Castle in 1976, by Olivia Robertson and her brother, Lawrence Durdin Robertson, an Anglican rector, to offer a multi-religious, multi-racial and multi-cultural base from which to honour the 'Goddess' of all pantheons. It is dedicated specifically to the Egyptian goddess Isis, because the FOI co-founders believed she 'best represented the energies of the dawning Aquarian Age'. Despite honouring pagan deities, the FOI does not consider itself to be a neo-pagan faith as Olivia Robertson explains: 'I would like to correct an inaccuracy in the definition of the Fellowship of Isis as a Pagan organisation. We are happy to have 1,000s of Pagans among our 21,000 members in so many countries. But we also have Catholics, Protestants, Buddhists, Spiritualists and Hindus as members.'

By contrast, *The Cauldron* magazine, also founded in 1976 by occult author Michael Howard, remains a lone voice in the wilderness of pagan waffle and represents an invaluable source of information for anyone seriously interested in genuine witch-craft and paganism. Most of the back-issues are now out of print, but selected reference copies can be viewed at the following national libraries: the British Library in Yorkshire, the Bodlean Library in Oxford, the Cambridge University Library, the National Library of Scotland in Edinburgh, the National Library of Wales in Aberystwyth, the Folklore Society's Library at the Warburg Institute in London, and the Museum of Witchcraft Library in Boscastle, Cornwall.

Nevertheless, there is obviously much that is buried in the Collective Unconscious. And if one particular element of tradi-tional witchcraft revealed how much interest there is in the pre-Wiccan forms of Old Craft it is the one described by Michael Howard in the Spring 2012 issue of *Pentacle* magazine:

In October 1964 Doreen Valiente, now regarded by some people as the 'grandmother of Wicca', gave the keynote speech to the first meeting of the newly formed Witchcraft Research Association in London. In her talk she said that the WRA was contacting surviving traditions of witchcraft that had nothing to do with Gerald Gardner, the creator of modern Wicca. She added that it was 'becoming increasingly clear that the old Craft had survived in fragments all over the British Isles.' Doreen was already aware of this fact because after leaving Gardner's coven in 1957, she had joined the Coven of Atho run by Charles and Mary Cardell, and then another traditional group known as the Clan of Tubal Cain.

The pedigree Robert Cochrane claimed for himself was impressive indeed and as Michael Howard observes: 'Today he is one of the most important and controversial figures in the modern witchcraft revival, even though he was in the public eye for less than three years before his premature death (in 1966). Having remained in the 'shadows' for 20 years, an original member of his group, Evan John Jones, revived the Clan of Tubal Cain and this new incarnation, under the guidance of Shani and Terry Oates, is extant to the present day.'

On another positive note, in October 2010, the Druid Network was given charitable status by the Charity Commission for England and Wales, which guarantees the modern group, set up in 2003, equal status with more mainstream denominations. In its assessment, the Commission accepted that Druids worship nature, in particular the sun and the earth, and believe in spirits of place; they decreed that there was no 'evidence of any significant detriment or harm arising from modern beliefs'. Being recognised as an official religion means that Druidry is categorised separately in official surveys and this could also pave the way for other minority faiths to gain official acceptance.

As Luke Eastwood, author of *The Druid's Primer*, wrote in an issue of *The Cauldron* (May 2012), it was only really from the second half of the 20th century that any serious attempt was made to reintroduce genuine Celtic culture into the centre of the of the Druid movement. 'Sadly,' he wrote, 'due to a huge loss of Druidic lore and wisdom, this process remains difficult.

However, widely reduced and scattered as it is, there is still a considerable amount of genuine Celtic remnants in the early literature, folklore and cultural survivals. Neo-Druidry is finally re-establishing itself as a genuine spiritual path ...'

Whichever path of magic or mysticism an individual chooses to follow, sooner or later he or she will come up against the almost tangible force field or 'energy' that occultists refer to as 'the soul of the world' – the Anima Mundi. The most simplistic approach is to describe this as Jung's Collective or Universal Unconscious that can be located in the inner recesses of the subconscious mind to the outer reaches of the cosmos.

Once we get past the veil of illusionary magical practice, however, we discover that all occult learning is concerned with the 'deepest and most secret aspects' of the human mind. Occultist Francis King described the Anima Mundi as 'being like a vast underground reservoir, not of water, but of memory. All humanity's past experiences, thoughts, dreams and hopes are contained in this reservoir, the contents of which are constantly being increased by contemporary experience'. Similarly, the psychologist C G Jung maintained that the human mind had been shaped and affected by hundreds of thousands of years of human experience, the concentrated essence of this being buried deep in the minds of each of us, shared by all humanity but in no way individualised.

Occult teaching is based on a vast variety of magical techniques, which enables the seeker to use one or many of the various 'astral doorways' to connect with the Anima Mundi for the purpose of mystical or divinatory exploration. These techniques access the archetypal imagery of primitive and powerful visionary experiences both on the inner and outer planes. As Francis King goes on to explain: 'Whether one chooses to call this 'well' of living images the collective unconsciousness, or the Anima Mundi is of no great importance. The point is that the concept is a significant one in relation to the whole field of the occult, establishing a connection between such seemingly unconnected occult techniques as dowsing and ritual magic, divination by geomancy or alchemy.'

This means that whether the seeker chooses the path of the shaman, Wicca, traditional British Old Craft, Asatru, hedge-witchery, Druidry *et al*, the tools required to connect with the Anima Mundi are universal. By using the different means available, the seeker can consciously establish contact through the application of pathworking and meditation. It may also goes a long way to explain why the religious and spiritual influences of ancient beliefs persist into the 21st century when science tells us that religion and superstition should have been rendered redundant.

It is unimportant whether these ancient gods, angels, demons or the Faere Folk actually exist, the point is that **the Anima Mundi behaves as though they do**. In this way, the vodun priestess, the Celtic shaman, the Druid and the witch all employ their own individual or traditional techniques to bring the creative force of the Universe into their own lives and into the life of the world of which they form a part. They tap into this reservoir of past-life experience and what we must also accept is that this Collective Unconscious includes the 'totality of human experience', both good and evil. 'In other words,' writes Francis King, 'the Anima Mundi is a rubbish heap as well as a gold mine; it contains not only beauty, wisdom and knowledge – but destruction, hatred and ignorance.'

There can be no doubt that the expansion of scientific knowledge has systematically led to a change in the way people in general, and traditional witches in particular, view the world. It is also important to remember, however, that in the not too-distant past, orthodox religion was still attempting to monopolise the natural world, as well as the social and spiritual worlds. As P J North observed in *People in Society*: 'The movements of the sun and the planets, creation, the shape of the earth's surface and many other physical phenomena have been explained by religion .... Today we know far more about the nature of evolution and would not attempt to explain the origins of mankind in purely mythical or religious terms. Our ways of thinking about cause and effect now depend far more on science than they do on religion.'

Having said that, superstition or folk-memory, is still – consciously or unconsciously – an important feature of many people's lives. This melding of superstition and religion has been described by N Abercrombie as 'the God of the Gaps' since the belief behind certain practices leads to a feeling of unease if, for some reason, the right actions are not performed in the appropriate circumstances. In other words, averting bad luck or misfortune by touching wood in certain situations, throwing salt over the shoulder if some is spilled, or not making the right response on sighting a single magpie. That unconscious but powerful folk-memory of our ancient ancestors *is* old and, as recent archaeological discoveries reveal, a lot more civilised than previously imagined, as archaeologist Francis Pryor has made plain.

Let us take the example of the British warrior-leader found buried in his chariot beside the A1 at Ferrybridge in West Yorkshire. Experts have been unable to establish how the slim, 5ft 9in tall man met his death 2,400 years ago when he was 30 to 40 years old. But the find has opened the possibility that the site of Ferrybridge may have been of great significance to ancient Britons, perhaps the venue for a mass rally. Unusually for the time, the man had good teeth and his skeletal remains showed no evidence of wounding or long-term illness. He had been laid on the chariot, which was buried intact, with many of its metal fittings still well preserved

At first it was believed that a huge number of cattle found in a ditch around the burial site, *may* have been the remains of a huge banquet to commemorate the man's funeral. But tests have shown that the chariot burial took place at the beginning of the 4th century BC, while the cattle (which came from different regions), were deposited in the Roman period, the 2nd century AD. Angela Boyle, the head of burial archaeology at Oxford Archaeology who led excavation said:

It could be some massive affirmation of their identity at a location which had tremendous significance in their culture. This site would have been venerated for generations, and had been used for burials for thousands of years; there is a henge close by, and there is evidence of some building, perhaps a shrine, close to the burial site. The burial mound of this warrior would have been visible for some distance and perhaps his life story was etched in the history of the people as a great leader …We know the Romans were not far away at this time, changing the only world these people would have known. It might have been a gathering of people at the grave of a revered leader from their history, calling for guidance or support in the face of the invasion.

Chariot burials were reserved for people of high status, with only 20 previously unearthed near Edinburgh and East Yorkshire. Strontium testing showed that this man originally came from either Scandinavia or the Scottish Highlands, while the burials had previously been linked to the Parisii tribe, who colonised the area from northern France. Dr Janet Montgomery, now at Durham University, added: 'For some reason these people came together here in their thousands. Our tests also show that the animals came from different herds raised in different places. These beasts were driven here and slaughtered for a great feast.' The burial ground, venerated for generations, may have been the last rallying point for our British ancestors facing the prospect of Roman invasion.

Going back even further in time, Christopher Tilley, Lecturer in Anthropology and Archaeology at University College London, introduces us to *A Phenomenology of Landscape*, possibly one of the most 'magical' books every written on the beliefs our prehistoric ancestors. Tilley puts forward the view that the architecture of Neolithic stone tombs acts as a kind of camera lens, focussing attention on landscape features such as rock outcrops, river valleys, mountain spurs in their immediate surroundings.

The key issue in any phenomenological approach is the manner in which people experience and understand the world ... It is about the relationship between Being and Being-in-the-world. Being-in-the-world resides in a process of objectification in which people objectify the world by setting themselves apart from it. This results in the creation of a gap, a distance in space. To be human is both to create this distance between the self and that which is beyond, and attempt to bridge this distance through a variety of means – through perception (seeing, hearing, touching), bodily actions and movements, and intentionally, emotion and awareness residing in systems of belief... remembrance and evaluation.

We cannot ignore these findings and remain in a protective bubble of romanticism created by fake-lorists and fantasists. The term 'earth mysteries' first emerged as a recognisable label in the early 1970s and was used to describe the inter-action between the individual and the natural energies of the landscape in general and ancient sites in particular. Unfortunately the modern-day pagan revellers who make the annual pilgrimage to Stonehenge to celebrate the Summer Solstice, may not be marking an ancient festival at all. The latest archaeological findings add weight to growing evidence that our ancestors celebrated the *Winter Solstice* there. Analysis of pigs teeth found at a ceremonial site of wooden post circles near the monument has shown that most of the pigs were less than year old when slaughtered. An animal bone specialist at the University of Sheffield University's archaeological department said that pigs in the Neolithic period were born in spring and were an early form of domestic pig that farrowed once a year. The existence of large numbers of bones from pigs slaughtered in December or January supports the view that our Neolithic ancestors took part in a Winter Solstice festival ... and a spokesman for the project added that there is no evidence that anyone was in the landscape in summer.

In the concluding chapter of *Frontiers of Belief*, anthropologist and author, C A Burland, observed:

Occultism has always responded to different attitudes, to undergo development and change, and I think it will adapt itself to the technological age. Already we have evidence of this, for at one end of the scale we have serious scientists becoming more and more interested in psychic phenomena and attempting to measure and codify the forces at work, and at the other end we have the computer horoscope. I am certain that as the machine overtakes the medicine-man, as it were, people will find an increasing need for a spiritual, mystical side to life.

And a final word from Michael Howard: 'Today more and more people are becoming interested in traditional witchcraft as an alternative to Wicca. It is a trend that would seem likely to increase in the future, although the Old Craft will always be rather an elitist practice. It has always been for the few and not the many, and will remain so.'

But perhaps we can go one step further along the path and quote the words of another great teacher: 'Ask and ye shall have! Seek, and ye shall find! Knock, and it shall be opened unto you!' The genuine Old Ways are there, waiting – if only you know *how* to see.

Summary

We should still be on our guard against those who would degrade anything that does not conform to orthodox teaching. In November 2011, the Catholic Church's leading exorcist went on the warpath in the *Daily Telegraph*: 'Fr Gabriele Amorth, who for years was the Vatican's chief exorcist and claims to have cleansed hundreds of people of evil spirits, said yoga is Satanic because it leads to a worship of Hinduism and all Eastern religions are based on a false belief in reincarnation.' Even reading J K Rowling's Harry Potter books is no less dangerous opined the 86-year-old priest, who is the honorary president for life of the International Association of Exorcists, which he founded in 1990. 'Practising yoga is Satanic, it leads to evil, just like reading Harry Potter,' said the priest, who was appointed Chief Exorcist for the Diocese of Rome in 1986.

His views reflect previous warnings by Pope Benedict XVI, when, as Cardinal Joseph Ratzinger, he was head of the Congregation for the Doctrine of Faith, the Vatican's enforcer of doctrinal orthodoxy. In 1999, six years before he became Pope, he issued a document that warned Roman Catholics of the dangers of yoga, transcendental meditation and other 'Eastern' practices. As anyone with a grain of sense knows, yoga is *not* a religion, or a spiritual practice, and doesn't have the slightest connection with Satanism or Satanic sects. And yet here we have learned men of the 21st century, still barking up the wrong Tree of Life in order to condemn any non-Christian practices as evil.

Official figures published by the Office of National Statistics in 2004, following the first national count of religious affiliation on the 2001 census, revealed nearly 40,000, including Wiccans and Druids, were *admitting* to being pagan; while the 2011 census showed that 'Pagans ranked highly with 56,620 adherents'. This was interesting ... since the results of the *Occult Census* carried out in 1989 estimated that there were 'over 250,000 occultists (including some 150,000 witches and pagans), throughout the

UK, in addition to the hundreds of thousands of people with a serious interest in astrology, alternative healing techniques and psychic powers!' It is extremely doubtful whether those 1989 figures have decreased ... so it's not surprising that there's panic growing in the Vatican and pagans can expect more damnation from that direction in the years to come.

The Story So Far ...

In the Winter Solstice (2002) issue of the pagan magazine *Verdelet*, James Pengelly made the observation that the future of traditional witchcraft was 'already seeing a gradual return to the shadows' in relation to the 'old initiatory systems like Gardnerian, Alexandrian and the Traditionals'. He also, quite rightly, pointed out that there is much more to witchcraft than the modern pagan acknowledges, and he believes that in the future people will have to search for the traditional roots of Craft as they did in the past.

Contrary to what many so-called modern witches believe, it should also be understood that there *is* an older system of Craft that has never left the shadows, and which has its roots in the pre-repeal of the Witchcraft Act of 1951. These groups have never been part of the publicity machine to popularise Craft, and have always muttered darkly that the mass publicity of the last 30 years would destroy Craft – not preserve it.

As an Old Craft witch commented during the research for this book, 'The original Gardnerians and Alexandrians are now saying that they don't want to be associated with non-initiatory Wiccans and pagans but that's exactly how Old Crafters have always felt about Gardnerians and Alexandrians. Our ways are not their way. We have little in common.'

In all honesty, there is little altruistic about Old Craft. It can best be described as having a tribal mentality in that it believes in protecting its own, but with no obligation to mankind in general. In view of the periodic backlashes, even in more modern times, this is not surprising. 'Trust None!' is the creed of Old Craft and it has preserved its secrecy by not divulging its rites and practices. No matter what a publisher's blurb may claim, there are no authentic Old Craft rituals, rites of passages, spells, charms or pathworkings in print for one simple reason ...

Any Old Crafter committing any of these to paper for public scrutiny would be in breach of their own Initiatory Oath – **and this still carries the ultimate penalty for treachery and betrayal.** Admittedly, there are excellent 'smokescreens' that may offer a *parody* of the genuine thing – but the essence of Old Craft remains firmly in the shadows, where it belongs. Nowadays, there are also a lot of people now claiming their antecedents stem from Old Craft but a few moments of conversation is enough to reveal that their roots are very modern indeed!

The late Evan John Jones, the Witch Master of the Clan of Tubal Cain and member of Robert Cochrane's coven, expressed similar sentiments: 'From personal experience, I've found that there are a few traditional groups still going but they are few and far between. Mind you, I'm talking about clans and groups that I know of and have met personally, there are others out there, I know, who still keep to the old tradition of keeping themselves to themselves. Broadly speaking, between the ones I've met, there are certain familiar stands but each group has its own traditional way of doing things and seeing things in a slightly different way to any other groups.'

Although there may be a variation in formulae from region to region, the underlying Mysteries remain the same and the only way to know about the Mysteries is to have experienced them first hand. In the past, there have been those who have used these 'regional disparities' to excuse any breach of etiquette or lack of familiarity within Craft circles. In fact, there are so many undercurrents and overtones that any 'pretender' stands little or no chance of passing themselves off as an Old Crafter, no matter how well read or widely published.

There should, however, be no doubt about it – that although witchcraft is not a religion (and never has been), it has an overriding spirituality that is extremely profound in its concepts and perceptions. Which is why it is apt to return to Alan Richardson's remarks concerning the differences between the more public Lesser and hidden Greater Mysteries. A wide diversification of these Lesser Mysteries have been appearing in books since the 1950s, often regurgitated versions of earlier works, where mis-information and misunderstanding have been promulgated as genuine traditions with ancient lineage. Michael Howard also reminds us: 'As Cochrane said (and few people understand what he meant), witchcraft is not pagan, but it does preserve elements of the pagan Mysteries. A subtle difference.'

We have now arrived at the point where there is nothing 'new' on the market, and there are an increasing number of requests for books on the 'intermediate and higher levels' of Craft from those who have obviously not yet grasped the basic principles of the Lesser Mysteries. This is why there is often friction between the traditions when a group refuses an Initiate from one faction recognition or admittance on the grounds that the 'marks' of the initiatory experience are conspicuous by their absence. To return once again to the comments made by James Pengelly in his interview with *Verdelet*: 'To find it, people will have to search for it.'

Research shows that traditional British Old Craft appears to be as strong and healthy as it has ever been, and it should not be assumed that its natural orientation is nature-worship, as in contemporary Wicca or paganism. Old Craft *interacts* with nature. This means acceptance in all its guises – 'red in tooth and claw' – as it has always been and many of its staunchest members are country people who still respect the Wild Hunt in time-honoured fashion. In Old Craft, they still refuse to sanitise the Mystery of the Wild Hunt in order to gain points in a popularity contest, otherwise the Mysteries themselves become profaned and sterile.

Just as this typescript was about to be downloaded to the publisher, there was some rambling discourse in the Hallowe'en issue of *The Daily Telegraph* (2012) by the dogmatic Germaine Greer, in which she asked why people should have adopted the role of witches when the penalty was certain death. 'The people who thought witches had occult powers were deluded; the witches who thought they had occult powers were equally deluded. Witches do not exist ...'

I can assure Ms Greer that I (and many of my kind) are *not* delusional, and to quote the immortal words of Jean-Paul Sartre: *'I am. I am, I exist, I think, therefore I am ...'*

Bibliography and Sources

§ Essential further reading

Chapter One: Echoes of Time and the River (Prologue)

Exploring Spirituality, Suzanne Ruthven & Aeron Medbh-Mara (How To Books)

Facing the Ocean, Barry Cunliffe (Oxford) §

Folklore, Myths and Legends of Britain, (Reader's Digest)

An Introduction to the Mystical Qabalah, Alan Richardson (Aquarian)

The New Believers, David V. Barrett (Cassell)

A Study of History, Arnold Toynbee (OUP)

What You Call Time, Suzanne Ruthven (ignotus)

Chapter Two: A Haunted Landscape (Pre-history)

Britain BC, Francis Pryor (HarperCollins) §

Facing the Ocean, Barry Cunliffe (OUP) §

From Stonehenge to Modern Cosmology, Fred Hoyle (Freeman)

The Goddess of the Stones, George Terence Meaden (Souvenir)

Historical Atlas of Britain, Nigel Sail (Sutton)

Late Stone Age Hunters of the British Isles, Christopher Smith (Routledge) §

A Phenomenology of Landscape, Christopher Tilley (Berg) §

Religion Explained, Pascal Boyer (Heinnemann)

The Secret Country, Janet and Colin Bond (BCA)

Seven Ages of Britain, Justin Pollard (Hodder & Stoughton)

The Seven Daughters of Eve, Bryan Sykes (Corgi)

The Sunday Times Book of the Countryside (Macdonald)

The Tribes of Britain, David Miles (Weidenfeld & Nicolson)

Chapter Three: Lux Æterna for Five Masked Players (Invaders)

Aradia, or the Gospel of the Witches, Charles G Leland (Deosil)

The Atlantic Celts: Ancient People or Modern Invention?, Simon James (BMP) §
British Folk Customs, Christina Hole (Hutchinson)
Britain AD, Francis Pryor (HarperCollins) §
Britain BC, Francis Pryor (HarperCollins) §
The Calendar, David Ewing Duncan (4th Estate) §
Dictionary of Celtic Religion and Culture, Bernhard Maier (Boydell)
The Dream of Rome, Boris Johnson (Harper Collins)
The Druids, Stuart Piggott (Thames & Hudson) §
Everyday Life of the Pagan Celts, Anne Ross (Batsford) §
A Primer of English Literature, Arthur Compton Rickett (Nelson)
The Roman Book of Days, Paulina Erina (ignotus)
Roman Britain, T W Potter & Catherine Johns (BMP)
Root & Branch, Mélusine Draco & Paul Harris (ignotus)
Seasonal Feasts and Festivals, E O James (Thames & Hudson)
The Tribes of Britain, David Miles (W&N)
The Witch-Cult in Western Europe, Margaret Murray (Oxford)

Night of Four Moons (The Dark Ages)
Beowulf, Anon verse trans (Penguin)
Britain AD, Francis Pryor (HarperCollins) §
Cunning Folk and Familiar Spirits: Shamanistic Visionary Traditions in Early Modern British Witchcraft and Magic, Emma Wilby (Sussex Academic Press) §
The Exeter Riddle Book, trans Kevin Crossley-Holland (Folio)
The Historical Atlas of Britain, ed. Nigel Saul (National Trust)
The History of the Kings of England, Geoffrey of Monmouth (Folio)
The Lord of the Rings, J R R Tolkien (Folio)
Mabinogion, trans Lady Charlotte Guest (Folio)
The Real Middle-Earth, Brian Bates (Sidgwick & Jackson, 2002)
Sir Gawain and the Green Knight, trans Keith Harrison (Folio)
Sociology, Broom and Selznick (Harper & Rowe, 1977)
Sociology: A New Approach, Ed. Michael Haralambos (Causeway)
The Triumph of the Moon: A History of Modern Pagan Witchcraft,

Ronald Hutton (OUP)

Ancient Voices of Children (Faere Folk and Folklore)
Folklore, Myths and Legend of Britain (Reader's Digest)
The God of the Witches, Margaret Murray (Oxford)
Myths and Legends of Wales, Tony Roberts (Dynevor)
The Secret Commonwealth of Elves, Fauns and Fairies (1691),
Reverend Robert Kirk (IHO Books) §
The Seven Daughters of Eve, Bryan Sykes (Corgi)
Witchcraft Today, Gerald Gardner (Magickal Child)
The Witch-Cult in Western Europe, Margaret Murray (Oxford)

Black Angels (The Devil's Brood)
The Black Death, Philip Ziegler (Guild)
Chartres: The Making of a Miracle, Colin Ward (Folio)
Conjuring Spirits, ed Claire Fanger (Sutton)
The Encyclopaedia of Witchcraft and Demonology, Rossell Hope
    Robbins (Newnes) §
England in the Late Middle Ages, A R Myers (Pelican)
Europe's Inner Demons, Norman Cohn (Heinemann)
Grimoires: The History of Magic Books, Owen Davies (OUP)
In Pursuit of the Millennium, Norman Cohn (Heinemann)
Magic in the Middle Ages, Prof Richard Kieckhefer (CUP) §
Malleus Malificarum, trans Pennethorne Hughes (Folio)
Malleus Satani: The Hammer of Satan, Suzanne Ruthven (ignotus
    press)
Chronology of the Medieval World 800-1491, R L Storey (Helicon)
The Observer's Book of Old English Churches, Lawrence E Jones
    (Warne)
The Pageant of England, Thomas B Costain (Wykeham)
People in Society, P J North (Longman)
The Spirit of Britain, Sir Roy Strong (Hutchinson)
Sex, Dissidence and Damnation, Jeffrey Richards (Routledge) §
The Stripping of the Altars, Eamon Duffey (Yale 1992)

'Witchcraft and the Sons of York', W E Hampton (in *The Ricardian*, March 1980)

Eleven Echoes of Autumn (Elizabethan England)
Alchemy, Diana Fernando (Blandford)
Popular Magic: Cunning-Folk in English History, Owen Davies (Hambledon)
Elizabethan Magic, Robert Turner (Element)
The Encyclopaedia of Witchcraft and Demonology, Rossell Hope Robbins (Newnes)
Europe's Inner Demons, Norman Cohn (BCA)
Green Pharmacy, Barbara Griggs (Hobhouse)
The History of Magic, Kurt Seligmann (Pantheon) §
The History of Witchcraft, Montague Summers (Senate)
Malleus Malificarum, trans Montague Summers (Folio)
Man, Myth & Magic, ed Richard Cavendish (Marshall Cavendish)
The Occult Philosophy in the Elizabethan Age, Frances A Yates (Ark)
Plays and Masques, Ben Jonson (Norton) §
A Primer of English Literature, Arthur Compton Rickett (Nelson)
The Sociology of Health & Healing, Margaret Stacey (Routledge 1988)
Virgin Mother Crone: Myths and Mysteries of the Triple Goddess, Donna Wiltshire (Inner Traditions)
Witches and Neighbours, Robin Briggs (HarperCollins) §

Songs, Drones and Refrains of Death (The Burning Times)
The Encyclopaedia of Witchcraft and Demonology, Rossell Hope Robbins (Newnes)
English Society: 1580-1680, Keith Wrightson (Hutchinson 1982)
Malleus Satani: The Hammer of Satan, Suzanne Ruthven (ignotus)
The Stripping of the Altars, Eamon Duffey (Yale 1992)

An Idyll for the Misbegotten (Ritual Magic)
The Atum-Re Revival, Mélusine Draco (Axis Mundi)

Aradia: Gospel of the Witches, Charles G Leland (Deosil) §
The Book of Black Magic and of Pacts, A E Waite (Soc of Metaphysicians)
The Book of Druidry, Ross Nichols (Thorsons)
The Complete Works of the Golden Dawn, Israel Regardie (Falcon)
The Egyptian Revival, Dr J C Curl (Allen & Unwin)
Man, Myth & Magic, ed Richard Cavendish (Marshall Cavendish)
The Occult Sourcebook, Nevill Drury and Gregory Tillett (Routledge & Kegan Paul)
Ritual Magic, Elizabeth M Butler (Sutton)
The Secret Lore of Egypt: Its Impact on the West, Erik Hornung (Cornell)
The Secrets of the Bards of the Isle of Britain, Dillwyn Miles (Gwasg Dinefwr Press 1992)
The Watch on the Heath, Keith Thomson (HarperCollins 2005)
Witchcraft Today, Gerald Gardner (Magickal Child)

Dream Sequence (Modern)
Coven of the Scales, A R Clay-Egerton (ignotus)
Frontiers of Belief, ed. Frank Smyth (Cavendish 1970)
Malleus Satan: The Hammer of Satan, Suzanne Ruthven (ignotus)
What You Call Time, Suzanne Ruthven, (ignotus)
The White Goddess, Robert Graves (Pelican) §
Witchcraft: A Tradition Renewed, Evan John Jones (Hale) §

Zeitgeist (Epilogue)
The Children of Cain: A Study of Modern Traditional Witches, Michael Howard (Three Hands Press) §
Frontiers of Belief, ed. Frank Smyth (Cavendish)
Malleus Satani: The Hammer of Satan, Suzanne Ruthven, (ignotus)
People in Society, P J North (Longman 1980)
A Phenomenology of Landscape, Christopher Tilley (Berg)
Sociological Yearbook of Religion, N Abercrombie (SCM Press)

Moon Books invites you to begin or deepen your encounter with
Paganism, in all its rich, creative, flourishing forms.